ELON MUSK

ELON MUSK

INNOVATOR, ENTREPRENEUR AND VISIONARY

CHRIS MCNAB

PICTURE CREDITS

12 Andrew H. Walker/WireImage; 55 Brian Solis/CC BY 2.0; 63 Paul Harris/Getty Images; 70 FlyingSinger/CC BY 2.0; 77 NASA/Bill Ingalls; 79 NASA/Joel Kowsky; 82 SpaceX/CC0 1.0; 86 NORAD and USNORTHCOM Public Affairs; 94 Steve Jurvetson/CC BY 2.0; 117 Daniel Acker/Bloomberg via Getty Images; 119 Simon Dawson/Bloomberg via Getty Images; 123 Rafael Henrique/SOPA Images/LightRocket via Getty Images; 136 Tony Avelar/ Bloomberg via Getty Images; 146 Samuel Corum/Bloomberg via Getty Images; 148 Robyn Beck/AFP via Getty Images; 151 Steve Jurvetson/CC BY 2.0; 153 Gene Blevins/AFP via Getty Images; 188 Angela Weiss/AFP via Getty Images; 189 Monty Brinton/CBS via Getty Images; 190 Rosalind O'Connor/NBC/NBCU Photo Bank via Getty Images

This edition published in 2022 by Arcturus Publishing Limited
26/27 Bickels Yard, 151–153 Bermondsey Street,
London SE1 3HA

AD006746UK

Printed in the UK

MIX
Paper from
responsible sources
FSC® C171272

CONTENTS

INTRODUCTION

In 2021, *Time* magazine crowned Elon Musk its 'Person of the Year'. The magazine's editors and leaders were not naive in their decision; they knew it would attract opinionated feedback from corners of press and public, both approbation and disapproval. But the article was vigorous in its defence of the choice. It acknowledged that Musk's personality could be a difficult meal for some to digest. But against that had to be set the world-beating scale of his achievements, many of which are literally reshaping the technological future of the human race, on and off this planet. 'Musk is easily cast as a hubristic supervillain, lumped in with the tech bros and space playboys, for whom money is scorekeeping and rockets are the ultimate toy. But he's different: he's a manufacturing magnate—moving metal, not bytes.' To prove its point, *Time* listed just some of his astonishing adventures in entrepreneurship and engineering. His innovations and companies have remoulded modern humanity's narratives on online banking and financial transactions, space exploration, the possibilities of multi-planetary human societies, clean energy, electric vehicles, solar power, energy storage, traffic management, tunnelling, artificial intelligence, transport, and much more. At the same time, his face and persona have become as familiar in popular culture as that of any A-list film star. His every life move, personal and professional, is dissected, debated and interpreted in the media, producing not only, at its best, well-balanced analysis and insight, but also some harsh judgements and critical feeding frenzies on social media. He is also, at the time of writing, the world's richest individual. As *Time* noted, 'Now this shy South African with Asperger's syndrome, who escaped a brutal childhood and overcame personal tragedy, bends governments and industry to the force of his ambition.'

When producing a biography of Elon Musk, perhaps the greatest challenge is partly separating fact from fiction – the overwhelming mass of information about the man can actually hinder clear conclusions rather than help them. Another issue, however, is that of separating what you instinctively feel *must* be true about someone based purely on their external achievements from how the person actually sees the world and has pursued those goals.

Probably the best barometer for measuring how the general public might perceive Elon Musk is his Wikipedia page, where the bare bones of his life are arranged in the most accessible platform. The opening three paragraphs of this page explains how he is an 'entrepreneur and business magnate', listing the companies and ventures with which he is most associated (Zip2, X.com, PayPal, SpaceX, Tesla, The Boring Company, Neuralink and OpenAI). It devotes a full paragraph to various controversies that have swirled around Musk, ranging from the investigations by the US Securities and Exchange Commission (SEC) through to his distribution of alleged Covid-19 misinformation. It also quotes, inevitably, the fact that Musk has amassed a level of wealth seen by few entrepreneurs in history: 'With an estimated net worth of around US$221 billion as of March 2022, Musk is the wealthiest person in the world according to both the Bloomberg Billionaires Index and the Forbes real-time billionaires list.'

The bullet points of Musk's life, however, only get us so far in understanding the man. As we go deeper into our analysis and narrative, we will certainly find a highly complex individual, but also one who possesses a quite singular ability to *think*, and to apply his thoughts and conclusions to the most intimidating real-world problems. Elon Musk is not like most people, but nor is he metaphorically on an entirely different planet from the rest of us. What I would suggest is that Musk is a man who, with admittedly acute brain power and an intimidating capacity for sheer hard work, breaks down the barriers between thought and action. In this regard, as we shall see, he has much to teach us.

CHAPTER 1
FROM SOUTH AFRICA TO THE USA

Going back to where it began, one thing is clear – Elon Musk's childhood, his parents, even his more distant ancestry, are anything but conventional. Here, perhaps, we unearth many of the roots of his later innovative and driven approach to life. In many ways, Musk's early years were not easy ones. But they were formative. He seemingly emerged from childhood and adolescence as someone energetically ready to defy norms and ignore predictability. He also went into his adult years apparently comfortable with the sensation of standing on his own two feet, exploring the world without fear or the need for external validation or guidance. Combined with a remarkable intelligence, it would be a potent brew of personality.

PARENTAL INFLUENCE

While Elon Musk has become indelibly associated with a version of the American dream, he was actually born in Pretoria, South Africa, on 28 June 1971. South Africa was, at this time, a place of both landed and commercial wealth towering over the most abject and adjacent poverty. The nation was framed both internally and internationally by apartheid politics, which imposed a rigorous segregation between black and white South Africans. It was a land, environment and culture that tended to breed toughness and resilience as standard. Musk's parents were no exception to this rule.

Maye Musk, Elon's mother, is one of the more striking characters in biographical parentage. 'Striking' applies both physically and psychologically. Since her teenage years, and to this day, Maye has been a working model, her evergreen beauty bringing her picture spreads in high-profile magazines (at the age of 69, for example, she became a *Cover Girl* model). She is also a successful dietician and businesswoman.

Like her son, Maye's life has the substance of a weighty biography (indeed, she published a memoir entitled *A Woman Makes a Plan: Advice for a Lifetime of Adventure, Beauty, and Success* in 2019), not least because of the mentally expansive nature of her childhood. She was actually born in Regina, Saskatchewan,

Elon Musk and Maye Musk at a New York party in 2012. Maye's devotion to her children and own entrepreneurial spirit doubtless had a contributory effect on forming Elon's character and self-belief.

Canada, on 19 April 1948, although just two years later her family moved to South Africa. Her parents were the most extraordinary characters, as if cast from an adventure novel. Her father was Dr Joshua Norman Haldeman, a successful and noted chiropractor, but whose profession played second fiddle to a life of adventure, which he shared with his wife Winnifred 'Wyn' Josephine Fletcher, a dance instructor. Joshua grew up in the Canadian outdoors, forging a spirit for grit, danger and adventure. His pastimes or pursuits including rodeo riding, boxing, wrestling, rope-spinning and flying – he acquired a private pilot's licence and a light aircraft to go with it. The 1950 move to South Africa was something of an impulse, rejecting what he saw as the political and moral limitations of Canada (Vance 2015: 34) and embracing uncertainty in a distant, colourful and spacious land. The fact that he had a family (Maye was one of five children) didn't dissuade him; he had expectations that children were quite capable of looking after themselves, if given the freedom and character to do so.

Once in South Africa, Joshua and Wyn embarked on genuine adventures, which on occasions graced the pages of national newspapers. In 1952, for example, the couple made a precarious flight of some 35,400 km (22,000 miles) in their single-engine light aircraft, heading up from Africa to Norway and Scotland before making the return trip. The next year, he made another aerial voyage with Wyn and his son Scott, a 12,900 km (8,000 mile) exploration of central Africa. In 1954, he achieved international renown when he flew the hard-worked aircraft up the east coast of Africa, then across Asia to the coast of Australia and back again, clocking up an extraordinary 53,000 km (33,000 miles) in the process.

In total, between 1950 and 1970, Joshua Haldeman flew across 80 countries and territories around the world. He held prominent positions in South African flying organizations, including being the co-founder and president of the Aircraft Owners and Pilots Association (AOPA) of South Africa and serving on the South African Air Navigation Regulations Committee for five years. He and Wyn were also very keen-eyed target shooters, both winning national pistol-shooting competitions and becoming leading figures in club and national shooting associations.

As if the Haldemans' CV wasn't impressive enough, they were also dedicated amateur explorers and archaeologists, the young Maye accompanying them on journeys into remote corners of the African continent. Joshua was particularly interested in finding the fabled Lost City of the Kalahari, and from 1953 made a total of 12 land and aerial expeditions, encountering many of Africa's tribespeople and much of its wildlife along the way. His explorations were tragically, but in some ways fittingly, brought to an end in 1974, when he was killed in a plane crash.

Maye was certainly the product of the unfettered and fearless ambition of her parents, and much of her undaunted spirit would be channelled into her own children. Maye was, of course, but one half of the parental equation. Elon's father was a local Pretoria citizen called Errol Musk, who met and ardently pursued the beautiful Maye when both were in their teenage years, dating intermittently until Maye accepted Errol's repeated proposals of marriage, leading to a wedding in 1970 (Vance 2015: 37). His parents – South African Henry James and English-born Cora Amelia Musk – were bright individuals, and Elon would be particularly close to Cora, or 'Nana'.

Errol was a practical man, forging a successful career as a mechanical and electrical engineer and a building project and property manager. Much later, a media story circulated that Errol Musk had been the owner of a South African emerald mine. The story even spun out to claim, in some sources, that Elon and his brother Kimbal sold some of these jewels in the USA to give them a financial head start. In 2019, Elon himself exposed the story as an absolute myth, explaining on Twitter on 28 December: 'He didn't own an emerald mine & I worked my way through college, ending up ~$100k in student debt. I couldn't even afford a 2nd PC at Zip2, so programmed at night & website only worked during day. Where is this bs coming from?' Maye and Errol provided, initially at least, a stable and financially comfortable life for the young Elon. The family expanded with the arrival of Elon's brother Kimbal in 1972, then a sister, Tosca, in 1974. His siblings would be important to Elon as he grew into the world, especially his brother Kimbal, with whom he would share several geographical and commercial adventures.

LEARNING CURVE

One of the most insightful pictures of Elon Musk as a child comes from the research of journalist Ashlee Vance, whose book *Elon Musk: How the Billionaire CEO of SpaceX and Tesla is Shaping Our Future* drew upon many hours of interviews with Musk himself. The impression is of a child with an above-average intelligence and an insatiable appetite for learning. He was, and remains, an avid reader, devouring both fiction and non-fiction, from Tolkien's *Lord of the Rings* through to the *Encyclopaedia Britannica*, which he read in its entirety. It became quickly evident to those around him that Elon had an extraordinary memory, retaining even highly technical information with apparent ease; retrieving that information rapidly and accurately became something of a party trick. It was a faculty that would serve him extremely well in his future endeavours and which is still an object of fascination for those hungry to boost mental performance. (More about Musk's mental abilities is therefore discussed in Chapter 6.) Across his life, Musk has also been formidably adept at self-learning – give him the books and resources and he will absorb the content with speed, without the requirements for external tutoring.

Even allowing for motherly adoration, Maye Musk clearly saw something exceptional in her eldest son, even in his early single-digit years. In interview, Maye was asked when she recognized that there 'might be something different about this little boy'. Her answer: 'From the age of three. He just reasoned with me so well, and I didn't know how he could figure out things.' While a strong intelligence in the young is never something to be discouraged, it can bring its own set of problems. According to Vance and other sources, the young Musk was something of an island amidst a sea of childhood conformity. Other students would note his mental detachment, Elon often lost in processing thoughts and ideas, and this could at times have an alienating effect among his peers. Musk was self-aware about the way he differed to those around him. In an interview with podcast host Joe Rogan, Musk remembered: 'I think when I was, I don't know, five or six or something, I thought I was insane.' Rogan asked why Musk felt that to be the case: 'Because it was clear that other people did not . . . their mind wasn't exploding with ideas all the time. It was just strange, it was like hmmm, I am strange.' Musk felt that his perceived oddness had to be hidden from wider society: 'I hoped they wouldn't find out because they might like put me away or something.' But at the same time, the racing mind held promise and tremendous energy – when describing his inner life to Rogan, Musk said: 'It's like a never-ending explosion.'

Soon, the young Elon would also have to contend with a wider set of problems. In 1979, his parents divorced. It was the beginning of some tumultuous times for the members of the fragmenting Musk family. Immediately following the separation, Elon went to live with his mother, as did Kimbal and Tosca, but after about a year he decided to move to live with his father; Kimbal joined him shortly afterwards. According to Vance, the move to live with Errol was partly driven by familial logic – Errol didn't have any of his children living with him, whereas Maye had three, and Musk said that this 'seemed unfair' (Vance 2015: 42). While much of the detail of this period is appropriately firewalled behind personal memories and recollections, it is a matter of public record that the time Elon and Kimbal spent living with their father was not a happy one. The patchwork of published recollections has alleged that Errol was a gloomy, tense and disciplinarian presence, one that fostered acute tensions with the two growing boys. (An illustrative example of Errol's approach described by Vance was Errol's response to Elon's stated vision of going to live in the USA – Errol stopped employing the familiar housekeepers and made Elon do the chores instead, as an example of what life would be like for him in America.)

Nevertheless, there were some positive inputs. Errol was a well-off parent, and the two boys experienced much foreign travel and an environment with plentiful tools for learning, such as shelves of books. Errol was also a man with an engineering outlook on life, and much of that seems to have rubbed off on his sons. Elon and Kimbal would accompany their father to building sites and there gained some hands-on skills – basic electrics, carpentry, plumbing, bricklaying. Although none of these skills would burgeon into a career for Elon and Kimbal, they did teach important lessons about practical problem-solving. To this day, Musk has a very physical understanding of engineering, pulling down the walls between theory and physical action. Somewhat less constructively, Elon also became an experimenter with homemade pyrotechnics, creating his own explosives and propellants through improvisational, self-taught chemistry, with some spectacular and doubtless alarming effects. It was clear early on that Elon was the type of person who liked to make things happen in the real world.

In 2015, Errol Musk gave an interview to *Forbes Africa*, and threw his own light upon the paths and capabilities of his sons. He explained that Elon was an 'introvert thinker', the type of person who might go to a party and spend more time studying the host's library of books. Errol presents Kimbal as the more socially oriented of the two boys, whereas Elon appeared driven by intense intellectual curiosity about ideas and possibilities. But one story has a particular relevance to the direction Elon was eventually to follow.

Elon's youth corresponded with the true dawn of the personal computer. Having been almost exclusively the province of government and business since their invention in the 1940s and 50s, digital computers achieved affordability and widespread public distribution from the 1980s, laying the foundations for a digital revolution that continues to this day. According to the interview with Errol Musk, when Elon was just 11 years old, his interest was piqued by the spread of computing and he asked his father about the possibility of going on a computer training course. Errol knew of an international computer event, to be hosted at the University of the Witwatersrand in Johannesburg, but which did not allow children to participate. Under Elon's persistence, however, Errol managed to book his son a seat at the three-hour-long inaugural lecture. Elon was under instructions to sit quietly at the side of the lecture, respectfully dressed in jacket, shirt and tie. At one point, Errol went off with Kimbal to get some food, and when they returned, the lecture had finished and Elon was not where they had left him. According to Errol, they waited about before going in search of Elon, eventually finding him deep in discussion with visiting experts from England. As Errol walked up to the group, one of the professors told Errol that the young boy really 'needs to get his hands on one of these computers' (Caboz 2015).

It was solid advice. Computers revolutionized Elon's relationship with the world. Even within the limitations of the technology at the time, programmable computers offered a seemingly unlimited vista for invention, and this clearly chimed with Elon. The first computer he owned was a Commodore VIC-20, which has its place in the computer hall of fame for being the first computer of any type to sell 1 million units. Compared to today's machines, its specs were almost laughably constrained – it had just 5 kilobytes of memory. Yet Elon dove into its possibilities with a compulsion that would become a signature trait. In just three sleepless days, he worked through the entire BASIC programming language course that came with the computer, a programme that was meant to take months. Notably, Musk remembered that his father was actually quite dismissive of the device, seeing it as something that was not for 'real engineering' (Vance 2015: 45). This perspective was ignored.

The full picture of the relationship between Errol Musk and his eldest son is still somewhat hidden in the shadows, although a patchwork of details and inferences have emerged over the years in interviews. What is clear, however, is that the alienation between father and son became total. In an interview with Neil Strauss for *Rolling Stone* magazine in 2017, Elon stated: 'He was such a terrible human being. You have no idea. [...] My dad will have a carefully thought-out plan of evil. He will plan evil.'

Musk took readily to computers, finding a logical home within their languages, circuits and outputs. Notably, in 1984 Musk developed a science-fiction game called 'Blastar', which ran on just 169 lines of code. The 1980s was a time in which legions of early computer adopters spent hours tapping program instructions line by line into their computers, the keyboard labour eventually yielding an on-screen game. The South African publication *PC and Office Technology* were sufficiently impressed with the efficiency and fun of Blastar that they published the source code, from which Musk earned $500. Blastar is still available today, playable directly through a web interface. Redolent of a 'Space Invaders' scenario, Blastar's opening screen has the leanest of instructions: 'Mission: Destroy alien freighter carrying deadly hydrogen bombs and status beam machines – Use joystick for control and fire button to shoot'. Even today (the author speaks from experience of trying the game), there is genuine playability and challenge in the game.

Computers would be an abiding passion for Musk throughout his teenage years and beyond, but it would be wrong to give the impression that the young man was something of a sequestered geek. In fact, Elon, Kimbal and a host of friends and relatives had plenty of robust life experiences during this time, not least because they seemed free to pursue minor adventures largely without adult supervision. It is worth reminding ourselves that South Africa at this time was a country with many rough corners, blighted by terrible levels of poverty, divided by racial politics, and suffering from one of the highest rates of violence in the world, a rate that climbed vertiginously during Elon's youth. Yet the brothers would make rail trips between Pretoria and Johannesburg (the latter, by the 1990s, was widely described in the press as the 'most dangerous city in the world'), where they needed wits and awareness to stay out of trouble, and perhaps saw a slice of life often hidden from polite company.

During his high-school years, Elon also experienced the self-conscious agonies of bullying, both mental and physical, over a period of some three to four years. Musk's distinctive mannerisms could paint a target on his back for those children who were less tolerant of anyone deviating from the norm. Some of the episodes of bullying were violent. In one incident, while at Bryanston High School, a boy crept up behind Musk while he was sat at the top of a flight of concrete stairs, kicked him in the back of the head, then threw him down the stairs, from top to bottom. (It should be noted that Musk moved through six different schools during his childhood, a fact that he admits made it 'difficult to make friends'.) This brutal opening action was the signal for other boys to pile in on to Musk, kicking him relentlessly and smashing his head against the ground. Kimbal actually feared for his brother's life. The injuries Musk sustained from this beating required hospitalization, a full week off school and later even some reconstructive surgery on his nose. Other delights of these years included the bully gangs beating up one of Elon's friends until he stopped hanging around with him.

Eventually, life reached a more stable plateau for Musk when he attended the Pretoria Boys High School, and the violent bullying receded. Here, Musk was a bright and engaged student, although not a stand-out one academically. Through all the distractions of teenage years, Musk's interest in computers remained undimmed, however, and he was selected for a school computer coding programme, learning languages such as BASIC, Cobol and Pascal. But as Musk moved towards adulthood, his passion for computing fused with another drive: a deep desire to move to the USA.

Musk outlined the way that these two mental draws interacted in an interview in China in 2014:

I should say that when I was a kid I didn't really have any grand designs. The reason I started programming computers was because I liked computer games and I played lots of computer games, and I learned that if I wrote software and sold it then I could get more money and buy better computers. So it wasn't really some grand visionary thing. But when I was growing up I read lots of books. They were very often set in the United States and it seemed that a lot of new technology was being developed in the United States. I thought, OK, I really want to work on new technology so I want to get to Silicon Valley. When I was growing up Silicon Valley seemed like some mythical place like Mount Olympus or something.

The fascination for, and desire to travel to, foreign lands is a commonplace yearning in the young. But it is somewhat rarer for such impulses to be tied closely to a specific industry, or at least an industry outside the performing arts. It is even more rare for yearning to become practical action, especially in a young man of just 17 years old. Yet this is exactly the journey Musk began at this tender age.

Keen to leave South Africa, Musk saw Canada as the key entry point to life in North America, not least because his mother's Canadian citizenship was transferable to her children, thanks to some recent changes in immigration legislation. Musk had an added incentive to head overseas in that it would enable him to elude South Africa's compulsory military service.

Musk began the long process of filing for emigration, using five months of this time by beginning a computing and engineering degree at the University of Pretoria. Eventually, the papers were all signed and confirmed, and Elon Musk embarked on a new beginning halfway across the world.

CANADA

Given the adventurous precedents in Elon Musk's ancestry and own background, it is probably unsurprising that his initially solo move to Canada should be heavily unscripted. His first port of call was Montreal in the east of the country. There, Musk intended to stay with an uncle, but in those pre-email days there was a lag in communications and on arrival Elon found that the relative was now actually living in Minnesota. So, he initially crashed at a youth hostel while he planned his next move. In Canada, he also had a second cousin in the province of Saskatchewan (the province from which his maternal grandfather hailed), and thus he took an epic bus journey of some 3,050 km (1,900 miles) to the small city of Swift Current, not far from the US–Canadian border.

Once settled at a reasonably fixed address, Musk's next priorities were work and money. Musk's future as the world's richest man was at this point simply inconceivable, and he has an experienced understanding of low-paid physical labour in entry-level work. His employment in the first months of living in Canada included farm work, log cutting and boiler cleaning. The latter was by all accounts the worst of the bunch, involving crawling into the boiler of a lumber mill and scraping off steaming-hot debris from the inside, exiting every 30 minutes to prevent death from heat exhaustion. In a notable testimony to Musk's tenacious nature, at the beginning of the week Musk started this job there were 30 men assigned, but by the end of the week only three were still hanging in there, Musk being one of them.

Although Elon initially emigrated on his own, his mother and siblings gradually began the process of shifting their home to Canada. Kimbal was the first to arrive. The close relationship between the two brothers doubtless gave Elon a boost. The brothers had a strong, dynamic energy flowing between them, a force that would grow into more developed plans and schemes for achieving success in North America. But Elon also reconnected with academia, in 1989 enrolling in Queen's University in Kingston, Ontario, back in the far east of Canada, studying for a Bachelor of Science degree in physics and economics.

In 2013, Elon gave an insightful interview about his time at Queen's to the *Queen's Alumni Review*. He described his time at Queen's as 'fun and interesting' and 'formative'. He explained that:

'One particular thing that I learned at Queen's – both from faculty and students – was how to work collaboratively with smart people and make use of the Socratic method to achieve commonality of purpose.' The reference to the Socratic method requires a pause for thought. It involves a dialogic exploration of a hypothesis or argument, the participants using a process of deeply probing questions not only to interrogate ideas, but also to expose the values, principles and beliefs of those in the debate. Participants in a Socratic dialogue, therefore, are placed in a state of 'productive discomfort', examining themselves and their relationship to the world, not just an abstracted concept, and exposing assumptions and conformist ideas. In this pedagogical tactic, we can see a connection to Musk's later advocacy of reasoning from 'first principles', moving past accepted logic and ideas and investigating a proposition or problem from the roots up. (For a deeper look into Musk's application of first principles, and other strands of his intellectual outlook, see Chapter 6.)

In contrast to when Musk was at school, Queen's revealed Musk's exceptional intellectual powers more clearly to those around him. Some of his student contemporaries remember him as stand-out bright, even among the capable individuals of a respected university. He was highly focused, reinforced with competitive instincts, but he also embraced the wider opportunities that come with student life, fitting in time for romance and socializing alongside studying.

Musk also began demonstrating an entrepreneurial aptitude. His knowledge of computers played out well within the tech-hungry student community, and he began to earn money by repairing computers or building them to order. Outside the college walls, Elon and Kimbal also pursued something of a networking strategy with influential business leaders. Driven by both curiosity and confidence, they would contact such people out of the blue, and persuade them to give time for the brothers to interview them. One of these contacts was Peter Nicholson, a high-ranking executive in the Bank of Nova Scotia. The brothers left a positive impression on Nicholson, the young men coming across as likeable, interested and determined. Through this self-made connection, Musk forged a connection with both Nicholson and his daughter, Christie.

A particularly formative insight came from Musk's connection to Nicholson. One summer during the early 1990s, he secured an internship at the Bank of Nova Scotia, working directly for the head of strategy. As a demanding assignment for the switched-on young man, he was asked to analyse the bank's third-world debt portfolio, to see what value could be discerned within the portfolio following some South American debt defaults. Evidently doing his job with gusto for $14 an hour, Elon unearthed something he felt could be a winner for the bank, and for anyone who capitalized on it. He spotted that the debt of certain South American countries was backstopped by the US government, and the difference between the backstop value of what were known as 'Brady Bonds' (named after US Treasury Secretary Nicholas Brady) and the actual value of the debt was such that astute traders could potentially double their money, all protected by the US federal government. Elon excitedly took the idea to his immediate boss, who saw the value in it and ran it up the flagpole for the CEO of the company. There, the idea was killed, the CEO reasoning that there was too much risk in Argentinian and Brazilian debt. The rejection was to Elon's intense frustration. He felt that the bankers were missing the point entirely, and equally missing the opportunity for huge amounts of money guaranteed by the US Treasury. He later told Ashlee Vance that this moment made him realize how 'All the bankers did was copy everyone else' (Vance 2015: 83). His disappointment quickly turned into the 'confidence' that he would eventually be able to take on the banks, exploiting their tendency towards conformity and predictable responses. Here was a pattern that would repeat.

CROSSING THE BORDER

Although Canada was, and remains, a country with a fond place in Musk's cultural outlook, he never lost sight of his original goal: to cross the border into the USA and place himself at the centre of the tech revolution. Furthermore the 1980s saw the foundation of the internet as a potentially revolutionary technology, it was in the 1990s that the revolution became a global reality, transforming the nature of human communications, retail and information/ data exchange. And much of this revolution was being driven from within the USA.

Musk's first step across the border came in 1992, when he transferred to the University of Pennsylvania, entering the Ivy League of American education. Elon would study business and physics, and he thrived in the upper atmospheres of debate and research, surrounded by minds often as enquiring as his own, although few could match his relentless work ethic. While at Penn, he made an important and lifelong friend, Adeo Ressi, a student who would later go on to be a dynamic tech entrepreneur and investor in his own right, also sitting on the board of the XPRIZE Foundation, funding technology projects deemed to be for the long-term benefit of humanity. The two hit it off quickly as friends and rented a large house together, a building they notoriously converted into an informal nightclub that could hold as many as 500 people at one time. This was a semi-professionally run operation – clubbers would pay $5 on entrance. An even larger property subsequently rented was similarly converted. As this story was related to Vance, Ressi was more the party animal while Musk, who appears to have been a restrained drinker, kept his focus on making sure the event stayed ordered and organized.

As something of an aside, it is interesting to note a little more about *why* Elon chose the combination of business and physics to study at university. It is actually not a common pairing, the worlds of science and commerce often sitting at a distance from one another academically, despite the value of fusing the two being evident. Jimmy Soni, in his book *The Founders: Elon Musk, Peter Thiel and the Company that Made the Internet*, refers to an interview with Musk in the *American Physical Society* newsletter, in which Musk opted to do business as a form of protective power-play for the future: 'I was concerned that if I didn't study business, I would be forced to work for someone who did study business, and they would know some special things that I didn't know. That didn't sound good, so I wanted to make sure that I knew those things, too' (quoted in Soni 2022: 62). Physics, on the other hand, provided intellectual rigour (he felt that if he could handle physics mathematics, then business mathematics would be no problem), but it also intersected with those profound questions of Life, the Universe and Everything (to quote Douglas Adams' *The Hitchhiker's Guide to the Galaxy*, a favourite Musk read), which held a special allure for Musk. In short, business was pragmatic, physics was important.

Penn seemed to be the ideal environment in which Musk could form and shape ideas that would later become central to his work as an entrepreneurial engineer and unbound innovator. During an address at Penn in 2009, he explained:

> When I was at Penn, I started thinking about what would most affect the future of humanity. The three things that I thought would be the most effective were the Internet, the transition to a sustainable energy economy, and space exploration, particularly extension of life to multiple planets. That's not to say I thought I would be involved in all those things. But as it turns out, I am.

The specifics of some of these interests were explored in several high-marking research papers while at Penn. In these, Musk worked at length on the possibilities for massive solar cell plants soaking up vast amounts of free energy from the Sun and how to use the energy efficiencies of ultracapacitors to provide power to all manner of vehicles. Such lofty ruminations are not uncommon at university. What is striking, however, is that all of these visions persisted as driving forces in Elon's ambitions, and later became realized in the world at the most exceptional scale.

It was in the summer of 1994 that we perhaps see the true foundations of Musk's entrepreneurial future being laid. Heading down to Silicon Valley, he secured two internships, both tapping strongly into his interests. One of them was at the Pinnacle Research Institute in Los Gatos, whose work focused particularly on the development and applications of ultracapacitors. These devices, as we have seen, had already caught Musk's attention. An ultracapacitor is essentially an electrical energy storage device, but one configured to hold very high electrical charges, release that energy quickly, recharge fast, and handle many charge/

recharge cycles. This is possible because the performance of the device is superior to that of electrolytic capacitors and standard or rechargeable batteries. The properties of the ultracapacitor make them particular suited to any application requiring repeated and sudden bursts of energy – as in the acceleration and braking of an electric car – but Musk had visions of these devices being applied to a whole world of future mechanisms and systems, from vehicles through the space-age energy guns.

The internship at Pinnacle Research drove and intensified Musk's enthusiasm for energy research. Notably, he also found time to ruminate on ideas about the future of banking online, not least the possibility of building a full internet banking service, incorporating not only savings and checking accounts but also delivering services such as brokerage and insurance (Vance 2015: 84). Few of those around him at the time took the developed musings seriously, not least because at that moment in history the full potential of the internet had yet to be imagined, let alone realized. But like many of Elon's early ideas, once it was embedded, it would resurface later. One thing is clear from any biography of Elon Musk – he doesn't readily accept statements that something can't be done.

But Pinnacle Research was not his only internship at this time, this was just where he spent the daytime hours. As evening closed in, he went to his second internship, at Rocket Science Games based in Palo Alto. Founded in 1993 by Steven Gary Blank and Peter Barrett, Rocket Science Games was a growing game studio, Musk joining the company shortly after it had received a $12 million funding injection from Sega Enterprises and the Bertelsmann Music Group. The company was an exciting place to work, known for the way it brought in talent from both the movie and the tech industry to produce some of the most potent graphics in the gaming industry, aided by the hardware transition from plug-in games cartridges to the more digitally powerful CD-ROMs. At first, Elon was used to write basic code, but that box didn't hold him for long. He quickly impressed seasoned coders and industry specialists with his irresistible package of skills and psychological deliverables – the ability to work impressively long hours without apparently fading or succumbing to stress; a deep knowledge of both hardware and software; independent problem-solving capabilities characteristic of the self-taught programmer. Soon, he was taking on far more advanced duties for Rocket Science Games, including writing drivers to support joystick and mouse interaction with the games consoles.

Also around this time, Elon and Kimbal embarked on a now somewhat famous road trip, funded by Kimbal's sale of part of a franchise he ran for College Pro Painters, the proceeds being enough to purchase a second-hand car, notably without working air conditioning. Now they had wheels, they embraced ambitions to traverse the USA, beginning their trip in California then driving up to Colorado, Wyoming, South Dakota and Illinois (Vance 2015: 64), on the way back up towards Penn, where Elon would start his final year of studies in the fall. While on the road, the brothers had plenty of time to freewheel through various architectures for business start-ups, including one for a new system of electronic health records, to improve collaboration and information exchange between physicians. A business plan was begun, but the brothers didn't feel the buzz from the idea and it was soon dropped.

Musk graduated from Penn in 1995 with dual bachelor's degrees in business and physics. By this time, he had both gained some industry experience through multiple internships, each directly relevant to key areas of interest, plus he had gained an exceptional theoretical education. It seemed for a time that higher education beckoned, and he was accepted to do a physics PhD at Stanford. Had he stuck to this path, it is interesting to speculate about Musk's future outcomes. But as history now knows, Musk dropped out of his Stanford course after just two days. Education was over, at least in its formal context. It was time for his first start-up.

CHAPTER 2
FROM ZIP2 TO PAYPAL

Elon Musk's ambition and engineering insight intersected with the rise of the internet with perfectly fortuitous timing. The first e-commerce company had been established back in 1982 (Boston Computer Exchange, which traded in used computers), but it took another decade before the next major online shopping experience arrived, in the form of web-based bookstore Book Stacks Unlimited. Incidentally, this company would be part-inspiration for the launch of a new online bookseller – Amazon. com – in 1995, the start-up headed by tech entrepreneur and future fellow space visionary Jeff Bezos. Although Amazon was initially focused on books as its sole product, Bezos was actually in the opening stages of a vision to build the 'everything store', an online platform where consumers could purchase just about anything they wanted.

Underpinning such enterprises was the exponentially accelerating use of the internet and computers among the wider population, both in the USA and abroad. With the advent of web browsers such as Netscape Navigator, and search engines such as Yahoo!, anyone with a computer could now start to explore the widening landscape of the World Wide Web. Computers themselves had also evolved, from the clunky affairs of the 1980s into practical, flexible, affordable and increasingly powerful models, driven by operating systems such as Windows 95 (introduced in 1995 as a replacement for the previous Windows 3.1) and Apple's Mac OS.

The cumulative effect of all this amplification of technology in society is indicated by the fact that in 1991 there was a single accessible e-commerce site, but by 1994 there were 2,738; just one year later, in 1995, there were 23,500. The rocketing growth was just beginning, however, and if Musk was going to make his mark in the new era, now was the time to strike. But first, he needed the idea.

ZIP2

Inspiration came in the colour yellow. During one of his internships, Musk had met a salesman from Yellow Pages. Viewed from the present age, the traditional Yellow Pages – massive, near-luminous printed business directories, hundreds of pages thick and listing thousands of local companies – seems of almost biblical antiquity, but for several generations it was the primary reference tool for finding local shops, goods and services. However, the company evidently recognized that times were changing, and the salesman spoke hesitantly to Musk about the possibility of companies listing themselves on a new online platform. While the pitch didn't convince Musk of the Yellow Pages proposition, it did trigger the idea for doing something superior. Joined by his brother Kimbal, therefore, in November 1995 Musk registered the company Global Link Information Network (GLIN) and began his first start-up.

The core concept for GLIN was that it would fuse an online business directory with searchable digital mapping, enabling the user both to find the business they needed and to get directions to it. Companies would pay to have their details placed in the service, which would naturally involve attracting them to the product in the first place. In the company's initial press release, there seemed to be some uncertainty over the name of the service – the *San Francisco Chronicle* reported that the 'new product is called either Virtual City Navigator or Totalinfo'. It was apparent that the Musk brothers were on a steep learning curve.

The funds to support GLIN as a start-up were meagre at best. Both brothers had sunk their own savings into the venture and Errol also gave a cash injection. Further investment ($6,000) came from the Canadian businessman Grey Kouri, who also acted in a mentoring role over the next few years of growth, providing the inexperienced entrepreneurs with sense checks on ideas and decisions.

With a very compact start-up team, which also soon included three salespeople, the Musk brothers rented a small office in Palo Alto. Even with the collective investments, money was tight on every front, and the start-up infrastructure was on a shoestring. At a presentation at SpaceX on 8 October 2003, Elon explained more about these early days of experimental entrepreneurialism, and told his audience not only about the austere physical conditions they endured but also some of the basic problems of getting people to understand what they were selling in the first place:

We started getting some interest. Half the time it would be like 'What's the internet?', even in Silicon Valley. But then occasionally someone would buy it and we'd get a little bit of money. There were basically only about six of us. There was myself, my brother who I'd convinced to come down from Canada, and then a friend of my mum's. And then three salespeople who we hired on contingency by putting an ad in the newspaper. But things were pretty tough in the early going. I didn't have any money, in fact I had negative money. I had huge student debts. In fact I couldn't afford a place to stay and an office [at the same time], so I rented an office instead. I actually got a cheaper office than a place to stay. So I slept on a futon and showered at the YMCA.

A further detail is that despite GLIN being an internet start-up, the company at first did not have access to Wi-Fi. This problem was solved by Elon coming to an arrangement with the internet service provider that operated out of the floor below; Musk literally drilled a hole in his office wall and ran an ethernet cable through the hole and down the stairs, connecting into an available router.

Founding stories such as these are important in order to set Musk in his proper context as an entrepreneur. Some start-up giants had advantages at the outset, such as emboldening injections of finance or the backstop of an already successful business. Elon Musk started with almost nothing and built up everything thereafter through the input of his own hands, intelligence and labour, and through the teams under his ultimate authority. The first employees of GLIN were somewhat in awe at Musk's Herculean capacity for pulling extreme working hours without complaint or deterioration in performance. Only a robust biology could maintain this regime, but it also appears to derive from a defiant intolerance for anything that even hinted at the possibility of failure. Any discomfort, any problem, any illogicality seemed to be crushed with a combination of iron will and long hours. Musk indeed once stated: 'My mentality is that of a samurai. I would rather commit *seppuku* than fail.' (*Seppuku* – the slitting of the stomach as a ritual method of samurai suicide.) The nihilistic military analogy here is absolutely pertinent – Musk will go to war with a problem, showing a pathological rejection of retreat.

Gradually, the infrastructure and the superstructure of the product were built, with Musk himself doing the coding. Two acquisitions significantly helped his effort. The first was obtaining a licence to an existing database of businesses in the San Francisco Bay area, home to more than 7 million people and experiencing a major growth in financial and technology industries. The second was free access to the content created by Navteq, a company founded in 1985 and by the 1990s one of the biggest digital mapwork producers in the world. The fusion of these two sources gave Musk's new product the spectrum of utility it required.

The Virtual City Navigator was now taking shape and making sales, the latter courtesy of the skeleton sales crew. But it was still a grind to scale up the business, and it was clear that the company would need a substantial gear shift in capacity if it was to punch beyond its start-up foundations. Everything changed, however, in 1996. The 1990s were a time when venture capitalists were hungry for tech investments, and valuations for start-ups could be soaring. One company on the lookout for new opportunities was Mohr Davidow Ventures, established in 1983 in San Mateo, California. Its modern-day LinkedIn profile description captures its mission across time: 'For 30 years the Mohr Davidow Ventures (MDV) team has invested in early stage technology-based startups that redefine or create large new markets.' Senior executives from MDV met with the Musk brothers, who managed to convince the outsiders that GLIN could indeed be the next big thing. In response, MDV invested $3.5 million into the company – now everything would change.

UPS AND DOWNS

With the multi-million-dollar investment from MDV, Musk had gone rapidly from start-up visionary to piloting a fully-fledged and established company. The changes ushered in by the investment were quickly apparent. One of the most high-profile shifts was that the company acquired a new and improved name – Zip2 – its platform running under the URL www.zip2.com. It also took newer, bigger and plusher offices, to house the influx of fresh personnel. Many of the staff were professional computer engineers and coders. Their presence was quite a culture change for Musk, who up to that point had been used to doing the coding himself, using his self-taught skills. Vance explored the tension between Musk and the new tech staff, the latter bringing what they saw as more efficient and professional coding techniques, Musk his powerful work ethic and also his visions of how things could be done differently (Vance 2015: 74–75).

But the greatest of the staffing changes brought about by the MDV investment was the appointment (under MDV's direction) of a new chief executive officer (CEO), Rich Sorkin, with Elon being moved into the role of chief technical officer (CTO). Sorkin had what MDV regarded as a more solid and dependable industry pedigree. An economics graduate from Yale University, he had first worked at the powerful Boston-based management consultancy Bain & Company before going on to gain an MBA from Stanford in 1988, then heading out to Silicon Valley. He had joined Creative Labs, a US subsidiary of the Singaporean company Creative Technology, where he headed up the company's SoundBlaster division – SoundBlaster sound cards became the standard consumer audio component in PCs during the 1990s, accounting for seven out of every ten computer sound cards sold globally. Put simply, for the investors, Sorkin had the track record that the young South African didn't yet possess, regardless of his other qualities.

This decision would go on to have major consequences for Musk's relationship with Zip2. It seems clear from the investigative work of journalists such as Vance that Musk found the appointment of Sorkin uncomfortable, not least because ultimately Musk is a man who seems destined to lead, with his hands on the reins of strategy. Looking at some of Musk's later reflections upon business culture also throws light on what he sees as the problem of corporate conformity, with its focus on finance and shareholders rather than product development and innovation. In an interview for the Theoxa YouTube channel, posted on 15 December 2020, Musk was asked to clarify what he saw as some of the problems in corporate America. One he identified in particular was the over-respect for the MBA:

> I think there might be too many MBAs running companies. There's the 'MBAization' of America, which I think is not that great. There should be more focus on the product and on the service itself, less time on board meetings, less time on financials. [. . .] What's the point of a company at all? Why even have companies? A company is an assembly of people gathered together to create a product or service and deliver that product or service. Sometimes people lose sight of that. A company has no value in and of itself. It only has value to the degree that it is an effective allocator of resources, to create goods and services that are of greater value than the costs or inputs.

This perspective comes more than 25 years after Musk started his first business. But thinking back to his views on the missed Brady Bonds opportunity, we see a frustration with the traditional corporate outlook to this day. MBAs, in Elon's view, are not an automatic signal that companies are competent and innovative.

Returning to Zip2, the changes in personnel brought navigational shifts in the overall direction of the company. The focus on signing individual business customers was rejected as too slow and labour-intensive, so Zip2 now looked at strategies for more dramatic and national scaling-up. A plan to make partnerships with major telecoms companies didn't find its legs, but the company began to concentrate on selling its software product to newspapers, so that they could develop their own advertising directories for customers. This avenue of the business found the money, with 140 newspaper websites developed by 1997 (Soni 2022: 70). Zip2's innovations put the company in the press, marking it out in an increasingly competitive field, contested by the likes of Microsoft, CitySearch, Yahoo!, Craigslist and AOL. (Google had not yet arrived on the scene but would do so in 1998.) Using the new Java programming language, Zip2 was more powerful and capable than ever, and included services such as restaurant seat reservation and digital navigation. Investors flocked to the company, including Knight Ridder, SoftBank Group Corp, Hearst, Pulitzer Publishing, Morris Communications and The New York Times Company (Soni 2022: 70). The first two companies on this list invested $12.1 million alone.

There was no doubt that the lives of the two brothers had changed profoundly and quickly. Gone were the days of cash-strapped improvisation and financial struggles. Now they were affluent and prominent, at the vanguard of the Silicon Valley revolution that was taking over America and spreading to the rest of the world. But all was not well at the top. Musk would have sincere arguments over strategy and implementation with senior Zip2 executives. According to Vance's research, Musk felt that Zip2 could do more to engage customers directly, rather than positioning itself behind the front of newspaper brands.

Matters came to a head in 1998–99, truly pivotal years in Musk's career. Zip2's market was becoming a hard-fought one, and the company looked around for mergers and acquisitions that might give it greater leverage and increase its imperilled bottom line. In April 1998, the company announced that it would merge with its major competitor CitySearch. Like Zip2, CitySearch was founded in 1995, also in California, and trod much the same ground as Zip2, providing an online city guide to businesses, services, retail, entertainment and more, supported by mapping and travel directions. The proposed merger had an exciting logic to it, as the combined companies had more muscle to take on a new Microsoft competitor, Sidewalk. (Jumping ahead a little, we should note that in 1999, Microsoft sold Sidewalk to CitySearch.) The merger included the agreement that the company would run under the CitySearch name, although the CitySearch CEO Charles Conn emphasized in the press that 'Everything about [the agreement] is the merger of equals: We can maintain the best of both cultures and the best of both technologies.'

Yet the merger would ultimately collapse. Musk himself swung against the deal and there were concerns about the financial profile of CitySearch and also about how the merger would affect the status and roles of some Zip2 executives. The failure of the merger brought turmoil at the top of Zip2. According to Vance, Musk argued with Zip2's board that he should take the position of CEO from Sorkin, but instead the board, disaffected with Musk, took away Musk's title of chairman and replaced Sorkin with the venture capitalist Derek Proudian (Vance 2015: 72). In essence, Musk had been demoted in the company that he had founded. There was a clear lesson here about retaining control over one's enterprises.

The real game-changing event for Musk, however, came in February 1999. Out of the blue, Compaq Computer Corporation offered $307 million to buy Zip2, Compaq attempting to make its AltaVista web search engine more competitive against the likes of Yahoo! and America Online. The offer was accepted, and a huge celebratory party was thrown. For Musk, however, the takeover was a clear sign that it was time to exit Zip2 and move on to new horizons. He left Zip2 with $22 million, Kimbal with $15 million.

There is no doubt that the Zip2 part of his life had delivered a tough but formative learning experience for Elon Musk, with insights acquired into management styles, corporate governance, finance, the nature of mergers and the direction of his own ambition. But viewed in the round, Musk's success had been astounding. In 1995, he started a company on a shoestring budget and four years later he was a multi-millionaire. Now his future projects would have means behind them.

X.COM

By all accounts, Musk fully embraced his new-found wealth, buying high-end property, a light aircraft (Musk had flying lessons) and a $1 million McLaren F1 sports car. The latter was notable because Musk, evidently comfortable with affluence and emerging celebrity, allowed CNN to film the delivery of the car. In the video (still available to watch online: see at https://edition.cnn.com/videos/business/2021/01/07/elon-musk-gets-his-mclaren-supercar-1999-vault-orig.cnn) a youthful and clearly excited Musk receives the F1, delivered via a huge, glossy truck. The video as a whole is clearly framed by public interest in the new breed of dot-com millionaires, typically young individuals catapulted rapidly into wealth, mentally attempting to acclimatize to their precipitous change in circumstances. Musk gives the viewers some context to what has happened:

> Back in '95, there weren't many people on the internet, and certainly most people weren't making any money at all. Most people thought that the internet was going to be a fad. Just three years ago I was showering at the YMCA and sleeping on the office floor and now I've got a million-dollar car and a few creature comforts. It is a moment in my life.

But Musk also appears self-conscious about what the new-found wealth means both for him and for the way he is perceived. He states, somewhat cryptically: 'My values may have changed, but I'm not aware of my values having changed.' Another presence in the video is Musk's fiancée, Justine Wilson. Musk had been dating Wilson off and on since their days together at Queen's University. According to Vance, Musk had relentlessly pursued Justine, a beautiful and bright scholar with a strong creative flair, and by 1999 the two were engaged. In the video, Justine is clearly overawed by the wealth on display: 'It's a million-dollar sports car. It's decadent.' She then cautiously adds, as if sensing the potential judgement on the other side of the screen: 'My fear is that we become spoiled brats, that you lose a sense of appreciation and perspective,' but she acknowledges that 'It's the perfect car for Silicon Valley, it really is.'

Evidently, both Musk and Justine were undergoing psychological and social adjustment to their new financial reality. But this did not mean that Musk was taking his foot off the gas when it came to further projects.

Connecting back to insights gained from his internship at the Bank of Nova Scotia, Musk's next target was the world of banking, specifically that of online banking. If Zip2 had taught him anything, it was the energy potential of building a business that was just at the beginning of a wider technological groundswell. Online banking was such an arena. The very first home online banking service dated back to 1980 – it was established by United American Bank, subscription-paying customers using a special secure modem to access account information. There were several further web banking efforts during the 1980s and the 1990s, but none truly disrupted the established over-the-counter models and adoption was low; by 1999, only 0.4 per cent of US households were using online banking in some form (security concerns were a big consideration for many potential customers). But the relentless growth of the internet meant that at the end of the 1990s most of the world's major banks were looking at how to capitalize on the emerging technology, and there were plenty of experimental start-ups in the financial sector. One of the biggest competitors for any start-up was NetBank, founded in 1996 and based in Georgia. To give an idea of the volatility in the sector, however, NetBank's stock price oscillated between $3.50 and $83 in 1999 alone. Elon Musk would also join the race.

The first incarnation of Musk's new vision was X.com, incorporated in March 1999. Musk had decided to maximize the disruption of traditional banking by offering an online financial services firm that covered the full spectrum of transactions: savings, checking accounts, loans, stock trading, mortgages and insurance. It was a supremely risky venture, not least because each of the separate fields of finance had labyrinthine regulatory complexities, plus the coding challenge to support the online infrastructure would be immense. He would also be pushing into the headwinds blowing from the world's biggest banks. But Musk has never recoiled from a challenge, nor was he reticent about investing his own money – at start-up, Musk put $12.5 million of his new-found wealth into X.com. (A quick note about the quirky company name: Musk not only believed X.com was a compelling and interesting name, evocative rather than narrowly descriptive, but he also felt that the growing market for pocket-sized computing devices meant that X.com was a particularly easy and fast web address to tap into a miniature keyboard.)

Recognizing that X.com was wandering into areas of expertise he did not possess, Musk built his team. He brought on board two Canadian finance experts – Harris Fricker and Christopher Payne – and former Zip2 executive Ed Ho (an engineer and coding expert) as co-founders. Other talented engineers, lawyers and financial experts were employed, often convinced to step into the high-risk venture by Musk's persuasive pitch about what was wrong with banking and how they were going to fix it. Together, the fresh team started to forge X.com.

It was not to be an altogether happy marriage of minds. Tensions soon emerged between the co-founders, and particularly between Musk and Fricker. According to biographers such as Vance and Soni, Fricker found Musk's public promises of developing a full-service financial institution did not match the reality of what they were actually managing to produce, and the challenges they were facing. Relations deteriorated between members of the management team and five months after the company was founded, Fricker made a demand: either he takes over as the CEO, replacing Musk, or he leaves and takes most of the rest of the team with him. Musk, never someone to respond meekly to threats, would not relinquish his position at X.com and Fricker followed through on his decision, taking much of the X.com team with him, including Ho.

Elon still had X.com, but now effectively had to rebuild it. He did this without deflection or defeat. Musk convinced more and more engineers and experts to join the company, while also securing important regulatory licences and insurances from the Federal Deposit Insurance Corporation (FDIC) to trade in key financial fields. He even managed to forge a partnership arrangement with Barclays Bank.

Despite the turmoil at management levels just months previously, X.com opened for business on 24 November 1999, the boss working 48 hours straight to oversee the launch. The new kid on the block certainly stirred up the world of banking. Through its online portal, it offered person-to-person, business-to-business and customer-to-business payments, a ground-breaking shift away from payments by cheques or over the counter. It was also aggressive about pulling in customers, offering a $20 cash card for sign-up and a $10 card for each new customer referral. There were no overdraft penalties. By early 2000, the company had more than 200,000 customers and were signing up others at a rate of about 4,000 a day.

X.com was on the up, but there was still trouble at the top. In particular, X.com's investors were getting increasingly fidgety with Musk in his role as CEO, especially as the company was heading towards an Initial Public Offering (IPO – the offering of company stock on a public exchange for the first time). Thus, in December 1999, Musk was replaced as the CEO by Bill Harris, who for the previous two years had been serving on the board of the accounting and tax software company Intuit. But by the beginning of the new millennium, X.com also had significant competitors. One of them was Confinity, a financial software company founded in December 1998 by Max Levchin and Peter Thiel, two individuals who would also go on to become legendary in the field of dot.com entrepreneurship. Initially, Confinity – who rented a small office space from X.com – focused on developing a payment system between users of PalmPilot handheld devices. The founders quickly identified that the PalmPilot system had limited legs for the future, and instead switched their focus to developing a new digital wallet system for easy online payments. They called it PayPal.

PayPal surged strongly into life, not least through its adoption as a payment method by the online auction site eBay, which alongside Amazon was a rising giant in the field in internet retail. Given its change in direction, PayPal was now a direct competitor to X.com (PayPal quickly moved into a new office, one not owned by Musk's company), and something of a commercial war raged between the two until peace negotiations began in March 2000. The two companies entered into discussions about a possible merger. It made sense. PayPal had a huge and growing customer database while X.com had more in terms of cash reserves. The merger was brought to fruition, and the new, larger company (running under the X.com name, as Musk was the largest shareholder) went forward, quickly securing major external funding investment and with a huge customer database. One key outcome of the merger was that Musk was restored as the CEO, Harris resigning.

The merger between Confinity and X.com had parallels with the troubled marriage between Zip2 and CitySearch. The two companies had very different cultures, bosses and approaches to technology, and the two entities (according to sources such as Vance) never fully fused into a single co-ordinated entity. The technological argument was particularly bitter among the engineers and management, with Musk wanting to take the company more down the line of Microsoft software, while PayPal employees gravitated towards open source Linux systems. There were also growing problems with functionality, with frequent web outages, plus the volumes of online fraud were unnerving. The finances of the company were also taking a hit, as costs escalated.

Vance describes what happened next as 'one of the nastiest coups in Silicon Valley's long, illustrious history of nasty coups' (Vance 2015: 93). The context for this was that back in January 2000, Justine and Musk had married. The marriage between the couple, who divorced in 2008, is a topic unto itself, and not one that will be recounted in detail here. Yet in 2010, Justine Musk published a long article in *Marie Claire* laying out what she saw as the 'truth' about her position as a 'starter wife'. From her perspective, she recounts being drawn in by Musk's intelligence, generosity and persistence. In the article, however, she also detailed what she regarded as 'warning signs'. According to her account, as they danced at their wedding reception, Elon said to her 'I am the alpha in this relationship', a statement that she said she 'shrugged off' but over time felt was said seriously. In later response to similar comments, she retorted 'I am your wife, not your employee', to which Musk allegedly fired back: 'If you were my employee, I'd fire you.' Whatever the truth of these statements, it is apparent that the couple had issues to resolve.

The Musks had married when X.com was running at full steam, and at the time Elon had simply been too busy to have a honeymoon. So, in September 2000 he combined a fund-raising trip to Australia with a honeymoon holiday, to see the Olympics. But even as they boarded the flight, Musk had a sense that something was about to happen in his absence. Here, he provides an overview in his own words in an interview with Max Chafkin:

I think it's not a good idea to leave the office when there are a lot of major things underway which are causing people a great deal of stress. It was a combination of needing to raise money and I had gotten married earlier that year and not had any vacation or honeymoon or anything. So it was a combined financing trip/ honeymoon. Anyway, we were away for two weeks and there was just a lot of worry. And that caused the management team to decide that I wasn't the right guy to run the company. [. . .] I could have fought it really hard, but I decided rather than fight it at this critical time it was best to sort of concede. [. . .] I understood why they took the actions they did – Peter and Max and David and the other guys, they're smart people with generally the right motivations, they did what they thought was right and I think for the right reasons, except that the reasons weren't valid, in my opinion. But it was hard to argue with the ultimate outcome, which was positive.

There is some detail we can add here. As soon as Musk found out about the management coup, once he had landed in Sydney, he immediately turned around and flew back to California. By his own account, he was reasonable when he met Levin and Thiel, and while he was naturally disappointed, he accepted that the decision had been made. He retained advisory roles, but the governing centre of the company had shifted to the PayPal side of the equation, as evidenced by the fact that Thiel changed X.com's name back to PayPal within weeks of taking charge.

(Fate seems to have taken a rough attitude towards Musk's attempts to take a honeymoon. In the following December, Justine and Musk decided again to have a go at a romantic vacation, this time a two-week trip to Brazil and South Africa. While on a South African game reserve, Musk contracted a particularly dangerous form of malaria, one that manifested itself in truly life-threatening symptoms when he returned to California. His condition was misdiagnosed by several doctors until one finally understood what they were dealing with. The correct diagnosis undoubtedly saved Musk's life, but it was a close-run thing, and he spent a total of ten days in intensive care. In total it took him six months to recover. He imparted a lesson from this experience to Vance: 'Vacations will kill you!' – Vance 2015: 101.)

Musk had played a driving role in building X.com/PayPal to the position it had achieved, with a revenue of c. $240 million per annum and hundreds of employees. It went into its IPO in February 2002, the share price opening at $13 but climbing to $20.09 by the end of the day's trading, generating more than $61 million of revenue for the company. (This was despite the fact that, according to industry analysts, PayPal had actually lost $283 million between March 1999 and the end of 2001.) Musk was still the company's largest shareholder, but even greater things were to come. In July 2002, eBay – by now a true leader of the e-commerce industry (by 2001, it had the largest customer userbase of any e-commerce company) – sought to buy PayPal, offering a prodigious $1.5 billion. The offer was deemed too good to turn down. From this deal, Musk (who was holding 11.72 per cent of the shares) received a post-tax personal windfall of $180 million. He no longer had control of a company. What he did have was a level of wealth that would truly open up even greater possibilities.

NEW HORIZONS

Throughout this book, we will have occasions to think more on the topic of Elon Musk's wealth, and what it means to be one of the wealthiest people on the planet. Extreme wealth does tend to attract a lot of media fire, and Musk has taken more than his fair share of spite and accusation on the issue, particularly over topics such as his payment of taxes. (One important point to note – in December 2021, Musk explained that he would pay $11 billion in tax for the year, potentially a record amount of tax paid by a single individual.) In a video shown on YouTube, Musk provides a considered thought on why it might not be a good idea to tax very wealthy individuals too heavily, because it relies on the assumption that the taxes collected would be put to better use by government:

Like, if you think of assets beyond a certain level that are far beyond, let's say, somebody's ability to consume, then at a certain point really what you are doing is capital allocation. So it's not money for personal expenditures, what you're doing is capital allocation. And it does not make sense to take the job of capital allocation away from people who have demonstrated great skill in capital allocation and give it to an entity that has demonstrated very poor skill in capital allocation, which is the government. I mean you can think of the government as essentially a corporation in the limit. The government is simply the biggest corporation with a monopoly on violence and where you have no recourse. So how much money do you want to give that entity?

There is a tendency to see billionaire wealth as equivalent to a massive bank balance, whereas in reality much of that wealth does not exist as ready cash but as the values of stock and capital. In Musk's vision, his wealth is an opportunity to make efficient and targeted capital allocations that governments either wouldn't make in the first place or which they wouldn't do efficiently, with all the cost overruns and wastage characteristic of so many public projects.

By the published accounts, and listening to some of Musk's interviews, his time at X.com and PayPal seems to have been a tense period, particularly in the fraught aftermath of the merger between the two companies. Many media analysts turned on Musk in their scrutiny of the affair, questioning his leadership style, the practicality of his ambitions, and to some extent his character. In some ways, the attacks set a trend – to this day, the media (social and conventional) and many corners of the internet are replete with invective against Musk, although Musk's willingness to retaliate against accusations reins in some of the extremes. Such attacks, however, can distract us from the sheer levels of achievement that Musk has attained in his endeavours, results that could only accrue through exceptional application of intelligence and effort to a self-identified problem. Although Musk, by one interpretation, ultimately lost control of the online bank that he created and ran, let's be clear about what he achieved during this time. With his own money, Elon Musk set up a financial services company that attracted hundreds of thousands of customers, became a leading player in online banking, grew through two major mergers and eventually brought Musk personal wealth that was more than 150 per cent greater than that he accrued with the sale of Zip2. Now remind ourselves that at the time eBay bought PayPal he was just 31 years old. It was an astonishing journey by any account.

Nor must we regard this vertical ascent to success as more a matter of luck than judgement. In 'Appendix 2' of his biography of Musk, Vance provides a transcript of an interview with Musk in which the entrepreneur defends some of his decisions and visions at X.com and PayPal. What comes across strongly is that Musk never relinquishes his desire to transform conventional models, but also keeps a firm grip on the intrinsic logic behind the innovation – everything is calculated fully. The phrase 'hope for the best' doesn't seem to be part of Musk's vocabulary, however risky the venture. Some of the key points he made are:

- He argued that the brand change from X.com to PayPal was not necessarily the wrong move, but if he had been present to talk with the board (rather than on an aircraft bound for Australia) he believes he could have persuaded them that the timing wasn't right. (Although he accepts that he might have made the same decision with the information the board possessed.)

- Switching to the Microsoft programming tools would have brought considerable efficiencies to the coding process, not least through the extensive support libraries published by Microsoft.

- To Vance, Musk defended and explained the financial models he drove at PayPal: 'Almost no one understands how PayPal actually worked or why it took off when other payment systems before and after it didn't' (Vance 2015: 406). Musk detailed how both the external automated clearing house and internally processed transactions promoted speed and efficiency and, in the case of internal transactions, protected against fraud. He also pushed the development of the PayPal money market fund, at cost, to encourage customers to keep their transactions internal to PayPal.

The full interview is recommended reading for anyone wanting a deeper insight into Musk's understanding of this controversial episode in dot.com history. But he returns to a core belief: 'The objective should be – what delivers fundamental value?' (Vance 2015: 408). This outlook resonates with that of one of Musk's commercial peers, Jeff Bezos, whose lifelong fixation has been to put customer needs above almost any other consideration.

So whatever interpretations are applied to Musk's actions and behaviours during his first decade of entrepreneurial activity, there is no doubt that he was a driving force in the digital revolution and established his credentials as someone capable of following his instincts for innovation to their fullest limits. Elon Musk has few ceilings on his ambitions, as was perfectly demonstrated in his next venture – he was going into the space business.

Before we turn to the foundation and rise of SpaceX, a tragic personal episode in Musk's personal life needs recording, not least to show that Musk's life was not purely one of challenges at work. Shortly before the eBay acquisition of PayPal, Justine and Elon had their first child together, a boy – Nevada Alexander Musk. Ten weeks later, Elon and Justine discovered him not breathing and unresponsive in his cot. Paramedics rushed him into hospital, but after three days, the life support machines were switched off. He had died from sudden infant death syndrome (SIDS).

A photo of a very youthful-looking Elon Musk, taken in 2008, although by this time he had founded or co-founded several multi-million-dollar enterprises, including Zip2, PayPal, SpaceX and Tesla.

Musk dealt with the grief in a very private fashion and has said that he is a person who doesn't 'see the value in grieving publicly' (Vance 2015: 123). He threw himself into his work. In her article for *Marie Claire*, by contrast, Justine spoke of how the death of her first child sent her into a 'long inward spiral of depression'.

The couple would go on to have more children, Justine stating that she went to an IVF clinic within two months of the loss of Nevada. In total, the Musks would have five more children together – twins Xavier and Griffin were born in April 2004, followed by triplets Kai, Saxon and Damian in 2006. The marriage, however, was not to last – Elon filed for divorce in 2008, precipitating a long and complex settlement between the couple, in which the public naturally took great interest.

CHAPTER 3
SPACEX

Right now, some 160–2,000 km (100–1,240 miles) above our heads, there are more than 6,500 satellites orbiting Earth. The number needs some context – only about half of them are active, the rest being defunct space junk destined either to circle Earth silently in near-perpetuity or eventually burn up with furnace fury as they slide back into the friction of Earth's atmosphere. So, there are some 3,000–4,000 'live' satellites out there, facilitating all manner of tasks from enabling our phone conversations to predicting our weather. But a major proportion of these satellites, and one that is growing on an almost monthly basis, are courtesy of Elon Musk and the company he founded in 2002, SpaceX. The Starlink satellite internet access satellites SpaceX has deployed into Earth orbit, according to data accessed in April 2022, number no fewer than 2,335, with 2,110 of those still in orbit.

The evidence of Elon Musk's engineering adventurism is now wrapped around our entire planet. And it's not stopping there. More Starlink satellites join the constellation seemingly every few weeks. On 9 March 2022, to pluck a date at random, a Falcon 9 rocket (also built by SpaceX) took 48 satellites into space (they are launched in batches rather than individually). Just ten days later, on 19 March, the 41st batch of satellites, 53 in total, was added to the constellation. The ultimate ambition, according to various press sources, is for there to be 12,000 Starlinks in orbit, and possibly as many as 42,000 in the future, giving every corner of the globe direct internet access from above the atmosphere. (Already at the time of writing, 28 countries are connected to the Starlink system.)

As impressive as it is, Starlink is but one element within Musk's SpaceX programme. Over the last two decades, Musk has transfigured the nature of the space industry and the expectations of what it can deliver for the future of humanity. SpaceX had developed the Falcon 1, 9 and Falcon Heavy launch vehicles for taking people and payloads to space; it has produced four families of working space rocket engines; it has produced the Dragon 2 class of partially reusable space vehicles for both human crew and cargo; it is even designing and developing a fully reusable super-heavy-lift spacecraft called Starship, which may well become the instrument of the colonization of Mars. Wikipedia's listings of 'SpaceX achievements' (17 April 2022) are a stack of 'firsts', and include:

> the first privately funded liquid-propellant rocket to reach orbit around Earth, the first private company to successfully launch, orbit, and recover a spacecraft, the first private company to send a spacecraft to the International Space Station, the first vertical take-off and vertical propulsive landing for an orbital rocket, the first reuse of an orbital rocket, and the first private company to send astronauts to orbit and to the International Space Station. SpaceX has flown the Falcon 9 series of rockets over one hundred times.

Note the repetition of the word 'private' here. SpaceX's history and programme seem more akin to the achievements of a national government-funded space programme, not that of an aspirational private engineer and entrepreneur with no professional history in astronautics whatsoever and who had spent the previous decade creating internet companies. Certainly, Musk was wealthy. But what will be clear from the following history is that Musk's foray into space was no mere idle indulgence, the plaything of someone with too much time and money on their hands. Instead, it is a rigorously conceived, planned, investigated and executed programme that reveals, perhaps better than any of Musk's other projects, his extraordinary capacity for treating even the greatest of challenges as opportunities susceptible to logic and process. On top of that, there was the added thrill of changing the model of an entire industry and the possibility of building multi-planetary life.

WHY SPACE?

We must begin with the question, asked of Musk by several interviewers, 'Why space?' The question is not just curious speculation. As rich as Musk was at the beginning of the new millennium, his millions could be small change when put in context of the costs associated with spaceflight and exploration. For example, a single NASA Space Shuttle launch was, by 2012, running at a cost of $1.64 billion. Launching an individual satellite can, depending on the size of the payload and vehicle launching it, cost anywhere between $10 million and $400 million, and this is not counting the cost of the satellite itself – a typical weather satellite costs in the region of $290 million. So, if there is any commercial sector that can burn through hard-earned millions of dollars at ease, it is the space industry. Musk would have been well aware of the story of Beal Aerospace, founded in February 1997 by

Andrew Beal, president of Beal Bank in Dallas, Texas, to develop a new heavy launch vehicle, but which ceased operations in 2000, having spent millions of dollars on development and testing.

So again, why space? We start with conversation between Frances Anderton and Musk on 18 March 2013, at Tesla Motors:

> The reason for SpaceX and Tesla – they are not really directly related but I think that they try to solve problems of importance. One is, in the case of Tesla, sustainable transport. We [i.e. humanity] just weren't making enough progress with electric cars and something needed to be done on that front. And then on SpaceX I just think that in order for us to have an exciting future that we can feel inspired about … having a future as a space-faring civilisation is an inspiring and exciting one. […] I do want to make clear that I am optimistic about the future of Earth, as well as I think we should aspire to become a multi-planet civilisation.

The answer Musk gives here feels like a blend of engineering pragmatism and sci-fi futurism. The phrase 'something needed to be done' could well serve as a mantra in Musk's life – if he sees an important human, engineering or commercial process being performed with less-than-optimal efficiency, he seems driven to fix it. His vision of the 'space-faring civilization' is more emotive, but rather underexplained, as if it is axiomatic that we should recognize the value of what he describes, just from its inherent worthiness.

Flesh is put on the bones of this vision in other speeches. When asked by one interviewer, 'Why do we need to build a city on Mars with a million people on it?', Musk answered with a heightened degree of passion, reaching towards something that could possibly be a core philosophy:

> It is important to have a future that is inspiring [...] There have to be reasons why you get up in the morning and you want to live. Why do you want to live? What's the point? What inspires you? What do you love about the future? And if we are not out there ... if the future does not include being out there among the stars and being a multi-planet species. I find that ... it's incredibly depressing if that's not the future that we are going to have.

Musk appears almost incredulous that anyone could not share the instinctual drive to explore everything that can be explored, and to investigate the very limits of innovation. Indeed, he followed this reflection with an assessment of the key landmarks in the history of modern space exploration, before connecting this history with something of a clarion call to embrace technology and those who pursue it: 'You are mistaken when they think that technology just automatically improves. It does not automatically improve. It only improves if a lot of people work very hard to make it better. And actually it will by itself degrade ...' Musk advocates passionate engineering as a way to counteract technological entropy, and to keep civilization making the best of all the possibilities for survival and growth, rather than just assume that they will come on their own.

Underpinning his technological futurism, furthermore, Musk also has a very clear logical sense of the challenges facing humanity. In other speeches, he explains the essential fragility of humanity, prey to phenomena such as extinction events and demographic implosions. Musk spells out the possible ends for humanity without alarmism or mythologizing, simply as rational possibilities and even certainties, based on mathematical and statistical logic. Essentially, we need to go into space because the risks of not doing so, and putting all our eggs into one Earth-shaped basket, are too great.

There was another compelling reason for Musk to go into space. Quite simply, it was time for a new project, and space seemed to have a unique gravity for Musk. Friends and colleagues noticed him talking and reading about the topic intensively, mentally downloading facts, principles, technologies and data about astronautics and the industry he was about to enter. Furthermore, there was definitely opportunity here. Until the 1980s, spaceflight in the USA was still largely a government monopoly, but the Commercial Space Launch Act of 1984 added the following to NASA's mission statement: '(c) Commercial Use of Space.--Congress declares that the general welfare of the United States requires that the Administration seek and encourage, to the maximum extent possible, the fullest commercial use of space.' It was the beginning of progressive deregulation of space in the USA during the 1980s, 1990s and early 2000s, such as the Launch Services Purchase Act (1990) and the Commercial Space Act (1998), which together encouraged the entry of commercial services into space programmes and broke the monopoly of the Space Shuttle in taking payloads into space. With the Commercial Space Launch Amendments Act of 2004 – by which time Musk had already founded SpaceX – private spaceflight was given the regulatory green light. As with Zip2 and PayPal, Musk saw that the historical moment was providing an opportunity seize.

Back in March 2004, Elon Musk demonstrates some of his early concepts for SpaceX. Musk taught himself the principles and practices of rocket science to an operational level in just a few years of self-study.

SPACE START-UP

Elon Musk's initial vision for space exploration was off-the-charts ambitious. He was particularly fixated on the idea of Mars colonization, although recognized that many investigative and exploratory steps needed to be taken before human footprints were imprinted in the red Martian soil. He began attending meetings of the Mars Society, a non-profit group of scientists, aerospace engineers and the occasional celebrity enthusiast (the film director James Cameron was a member), together dedicated to discussing all matters Mars. Within the society, Musk found a home for his ideas, while the society itself received a wealthy supporter prepared to donate money to projects. Soon, Musk was on the society's board of directors. But as his own ideas sharpened, and his contact list grew, Musk needed to move ideas beyond the thought bubble. He therefore resigned from the Mars Society and set up the Life to Mars Foundation, essentially a think tank and project group, packed with high-end experts, aiming to define and take the first tiny steps on the empty black road to Mars.

Reporting on the foundation's activities in September 2001, the website Spaceref.com celebrated the move and outlined some of its programmes: 'Someone is putting his money where my mouth has been. Describing permanent settlement of Mars as "a positive, constructive, inspirational goal, capable of uniting humanity at a critical time," dot-com entrepreneur Elon Musk has pledged a substantial portion of his personal fortune to realizing that goal, beginning with a proposed $20 million technology-demonstration Mars lander to be launched perhaps in 2005.'

More specifically, Musk's ideas for Mars exploration consolidated into two main strands within the group, both of which could be regarded as adventurous or kooky, depending on your outlook. First, as a feasibility study, he wanted to send mice to Mars and bring them back again. Second came the idea for a 'Mars Oasis', in which a robotic greenhouse would be deployed to the Martian landscape. The greenhouse would be used to grow plants, not only testing the possibilities of establishing a basic agriculture for future human inhabitants, but also generating oxygen within the Martian atmosphere.

Ideas were one thing; reality was another entirely. The scientists and aerospace engineers were especially concerned about the limitations of Elon's $20–30 million budget, which from their experience could be gobbled up quickly in hefty, voracious bites by even quite a humble space programme. For Musk, therefore, an immediate priority was to acquire budget rocketry, and for that he looked to Russia. Specifically, he intended to buy Russian intercontinental ballistic missiles (ICBMs), seeking an off-the-shelf affordability, and repurpose them for spaceflight.

In the autumn of 2001, Musk travelled to Russia on a buying mission, accompanied by veteran space engineer Jim Cantrell and Musk's former university friend Adeo Ressi, who by now was a successful multi-millionaire entrepreneur in his own right. By all accounts, the trips were awkward and frustrating affairs for Musk, the Russian representatives failing to take Musk's proposals seriously, and seeing the meetings more as adjuncts to vodka shots. The team went to Russia again in February 2002, this time taking with them Mike Griffin, who had previously worked for In-Q-Tel (a venture capital arm of the CIA), NASA's Jet Propulsion Laboratory (JPL) and aerospace company Orbital Sciences. The negotiations were similarly rough and ready affairs, but the Russian dealers fell short of the right price for Musk – they offered the missiles for $8 million each; Musk wanted two for that price. Eventually, the US teams found themselves on the return flight to the USA, their shopping basket empty.

An impressive moment in the history of Musk's journey to space now occurred. A dispirited team sat on the return flight, turning over their own thoughts while many also reached for the glasses of alcohol. Not Musk. He sat on his own, hunched over his laptop and typing fast and hard into a spreadsheet. This activity went on for some time until eventually Musk turned back to the group and announced that he had found a solution to the problem of sourcing and affording the rockets: 'I think we can build this rocket ourselves' (Vance 2015: 107). It was an extraordinary claim, and one that many in the group initially regarded as fantastical, an optimal way for Musk to scythe through his substantial financial resources. Once Musk had passed around his laptop, however, the reticence turned to interest. In the spreadsheet, Musk had modelled in detail, and with accuracy and a clearly considerable knowledge, the costs and materials involved in his space company manufacturing its own powerplants, and even included some calculations of performance characteristics. He had also revised his vision. His ambitions to reach Mars would be parked, albeit temporarily. Instead, he would specifically focus on the development of launch systems capable of handling the new, smaller generations of satellites and payloads that seemed to define the future of space commerce, rather than the top end of heavy launch that had traditionally been handled by NASA and the major international space agencies. In the process, he wanted to make spaceflight cheaper and more efficient. He desired to become what he later described to employees as the 'Southwest Airlines of Space', servicing clients such as the Department of Defense, NASA and big communications companies for a fraction of the cost they were currently, and possibly complacently, paying. The astonishing feat for those present was that a self-taught enthusiast was proving a lofty elevator pitch with practical data and method. If anyone was going to argue with Musk, they would have to argue with hard facts and developed specifications, not with generalities.

Space Exploration Technologies Corps. – better known by its SpaceX abbreviation – was founded on 14 March 2002. Musk began building up a small, but steadily growing, team around him. One of the central figures of this team was Tom Mueller, a lifelong and brilliant rocket engineer and rocket engine designer, who had previously worked for 15 years at aerospace conglomerate TRW Inc. As one of the founding employees of SpaceX, Mueller shouldered the responsibility for developing the liquid-fuel rocket engines for several series of SpaceX launch vehicles, as well as altitude-control thrusters for the Dragon spacecraft. The others who steadily came on board perfectly fitted the Musk mould. They were hard-working, often young, with a demonstrably innovative spirit, and typically fired up about working on something new and cutting edge, liberated from the traditions and inertia of many of the corporate environments they had come from. Musk personally oversaw the recruitment; many bewildered engineers had phone calls or personal visits from Musk, the former sometimes thinking that they were being pranked, given the likelihood of an out-of-the-blue call from a multi-millionaire wanting to go to space. Over the next months and years, they would need all their energy and ideas to keep up with their hyper-demanding boss – 60-, 80-, 100-hour weeks would not be uncommon. But the accounts of members of this early team evoke a sense of missionary zeal and *esprit de corps*, as they found themselves participating in an electrifying mission, and given freedom to explore the full capacity of their engineering talents.

The early days of SpaceX had a distinctly improvisational feel to them. The company set up in a large industrial unit in El Segundo, Los Angeles, the space quickly filling up with desks, computers, workshops and engineering equipment. Teams of engineers would also head out to remote test facilities to conduct various engine trials; eventually SpaceX bought its own 121-hectare (300-acre) Rocket Development and Test Facility in McGregor, Texas, the site having previously been used by Beal Aerospace, who conveniently had left several big-ticket pieces of engine testing infrastructure. The SpaceX engineers found themselves oscillating frequently between California and Texas (sometimes Musk even gave them use of his private plane to cut down on the travel time).

The initial programme laid down for SpaceX was fantastically tight and ambitious by space industry standards. The core objective was to develop the Falcon 1 rocket (the name was a fond reference to the *Star Wars* spaceship the *Millennium Falcon*), a small-lift launch vehicle capable of raising a 635 kg (1,400 lb) payload for a $6.9 million cost, a fraction of the typical price of a payload launch in the existing market. By way of comparison, between 1970 and 2000, the average cost to launch a kilogram of payload into space was $18,500; based on the Falcon 1 model, a kilogram of payload could be lifted for just $4,928. The timeline set by Musk was hair-whitening – early presentational materials committed to launching Falcon 1 just 15 months after the company was founded, and this timeline included designing and building the engines, constructing the rocket body and developing a launch pad facility, plus gaining all the relevant regulatory paperwork and permissions.

Musk was physically committed in his approach to SpaceX. Designated chief engineer, he was fully present in the workshop spaces and test areas, observing, analysing, asking questions. He would also do hands-on work, getting fine clothes filthy alongside the engineers to get a job done. From first-person accounts, we build up a picture of a boss who exercised both patience and impatience in equal measure – he often accepted inevitable setbacks with composure, allowing the team to learn and move on without dwelling in defeatism for long. But he maintained a heavy pressure to hit goals and would not tolerate woolly thinking. Vance recounts the experience of former Boeing aerospace engineer Jeremy Hollman informing Musk about (another) engine test failure. Elon asked when the component could be operational again, but Hollman did not have an immediate answer. Musk pounced on this hesitancy, telling him, 'You need to. This is important to the company. Everything is riding on this. Why don't you have an answer?' Hollman remembered that from this point on, he always focused on ensuring he had information at the ready (Vance 2015: 132). Given the pressures that Musk himself was under at this time, however (note that by February 2004, he was also the chairman and largest shareholder of the Tesla company), Musk appointed a formidable assistant, Mary Beth Brown, who acted as a gatekeeper between him and those who wanted to take a slice of his time and energy. Brown became integral to the way Musk ran his affairs at SpaceX.

The most consuming aspect of SpaceX's work in its first months and years was development of the Merlin and Kestrel engine types for Falcon 1. Spacecraft lift engines have to deliver enormous but stable thrust over extended durations, and the sheer violence of their physics makes them apt to blow up with terrifying unpredictability during development phases. SpaceX's experience was no different, and the testing cycle was frequently an exercise in frustration and trips back to the drawing board. Nor was Falcon 1 the only project in development. Quickly, SpaceX began work on the Falcon 5 launch vehicle, which had an intermediate lift capability, although by 2005 this had been dropped in favour of the Falcon 9 reusable medium lift vehicle, which would be capable of taking up to 22,800 kg (50,265 lb) to orbit, powered by nine Merlin engines in its first stage (like Falcon 1, it was a two-stage rocket). The three-stage Falcon 9 Heavy launch vehicle, intended to haul up to 2 tons to low Earth orbit, was also in concept stage by 2005 (although the actual intention to develop this was not unveiled to the public until 2011).

SpaceX was tackling the heavily layered demands of a start-up space programme but with a constant eye to breaking traditions, working from the 'first principles' thinking that is characteristic of Musk's approach to problem-solving (see Chapter 6). The company was employing the principle of 'vertical integration', keeping as

Elon Musk of SpaceX gives details on Falcon 9 launch vehicles and Dragon manned spacecraft at the Mars Society Conference in 2006. It was at the Mars Society in the early 2000s that Musk really began publicly voicing his interest in practical space exploration.

many of the production, development and engineering processes contained within the company infrastructure, rather than fielding them out to external contractors; the heavy outsourcing of development to contractors was a major cause of cost overruns in traditional space development programmes. The engineers were encouraged to use as many off-the-shelf components as they could to reduce costs and speed up progress. For example, in the later production of the Dragon spacecraft and the Falcon 9 lift vehicle, the SpaceX engineers built their own avionics platforms from scratch, for a price tag of $10,000 – traditionally a space avionics system might cost about $10 million to produce. When SpaceX did use contractors, Musk would keep a gimlet eye on their efforts, sometimes making long flights for unannounced visits at unsociable hours, and expressing anger if he didn't find the contractors working flat out to hit the deadlines.

HARD TIMES

By December 2006, by which time an estimated development spend of $90–100 million had been incurred, Falcon 1 was finally ready for launch. (A previous launch intended for 19 December 2005 had to be abandoned because of structural damage caused by a faulty engine valve.) The pressure was on in so many ways. Not only was the vehicle running well behind the originally pitched schedule, on account of a broad array of technical and practical obstacles, but the rocket also had customers in waiting. The first two Falcon 1 launches had been paid for by the US Air Force and the Defense Advanced Research Projects Agency (DARPA) as an evaluation programme for new launch vehicles. SpaceX had also been given a $15 million contract for the deployment of TacSat-1; an experimental satellite built by the US Naval Research Laboratory (NRL). (TacSat-1 was meant to be taken into orbit aboard Falcon 1's sixth launch, but delays in the Falcon 1 programme and the successful launch of the successor, TacSat-2, on an Orbital Sciences Minotaur I on 16 December 2006 meant that the contract was cancelled.) A SpaceX 'June 2005 through September 2005 Update' to the press listed its customer manifest for future Falcon 1 and Falcon 9 launches, and they included the US Department of Defense, the 'US Government', Malaysia's Astronautic Technology Sdn Bhd (ATSB), Bigelow Aerospace, MDA Corp., the Swedish Space Corp. and the US Air Force. The same press release also hammered home the news about the value on offer for commercial customers:

> We have also changed our pricing policy to reflect the all inclusive price of launch to make things really clear. Some people were under the impression that range and 3rd party insurance costs were millions of dollars. Everything is now included, unless you have a really complex spacecraft or require an outside mission assurance process, and it is the same price we've had since 2002 – $5.9M for the vehicle plus $0.8M for the launch range, 3rd party insurance and payload integration.

With much riding on a successful launch, Falcon 1 roared into life for its first mission on 23 March 2006 at 22.30 from a launch site on Omelek Island, part of the Kwajalein Atoll in the Marshall Islands. Thirty-three seconds into the flight, there was a catastrophic engine failure, with the loss of the vehicle. It was a body blow for the team, after so much intensive activity and mental expectation, but they immediately made investigations to identify and remedy the problem. A second flight was scheduled for January 2007, but technical problems caused the launch to be postponed on multiple occasions before the Falcon 1 again lifted off on 21 March 2007 at 01.10 GMT, carrying a DemoSat payload (a boilerplate satellite used for testing) for DARPA and NASA. This time, the rocket reached an altitude of 289 km (180 miles), but then suffered flight stability issues and the shutdown of its second-stage engine, and failed to reach the velocity required to enter orbit. Although SpaceX publicly celebrated the fact that the flight had flight-proven 95 per cent of the rocket's systems, it still fell short of the intended success. The third Falcon 1 mission attempt came on 3 August 2008. Again, it was a disappointment – the rocket failed to reach orbit, following a collision between the first and second stages of the rocket on their separation.

The first three failed missions of Falcon 1 were grievous blows to the SpaceX staff. Morale was hitting rock bottom. Musk, a man of singular resistance to stress, was apparently emotionally assaulted by the trials of getting into space. He was reportedly 'waking from nightmares, screaming and in physical pain' (Berger 2021: 216). To Vance, he confessed to being 'super depressed' at this time. But Musk's problems at SpaceX were part of a far wider series of mental assaults. By the summer of 2008, the world was deep within the most devastating global financial crisis since the Great Depression. Banks and mortgage brokers were collapsing, investment portfolios plunged in value, millions lost their jobs. In the midst of this turmoil, Musk was not only running SpaceX, which had by now burned through $100 million of his own money, but his other major business, Tesla, was also on its knees (see Chapter 4). Soon, Musk would be fighting for financial survival.

On top of the corporate and technological problems, 2008 was also proving to be a harsh one personally for Musk. He now had something of a global celebrity status alongside his reputation as a businessman, as he rubbed shoulders with the well-publicized rich and the famous, all under the strobing flash guns and rolling cameras of the world's media. It was the year in which he was getting divorced, with all the attention and scrutiny that came with it. He had started a new relationship, with the English actress Talulah Riley, which did little to dim the public attention. (The couple would be married in Scotland in 2010.) The world's business press was also giving Musk a hard time, some delighting over his struggles and questioning his credentials for further success. Musk had much to prove, therefore, but he also had to survive psychologically. In an interview with Scott Pelley for CBS News' *60 Minutes* programme on 30 March 2014, he confessed that 2008 was 'definitely the worst year of my life'. He added: 'I remember waking up the Sunday before Christmas in 2008, and thinking to myself, "Man, I never thought I was someone who could ever be capable of a nervous breakdown." I felt this is the closest I've ever come, because it seemed...pretty dark.'

A moment of much-awaited light came on 28 September 2008, when Falcon 1 achieved its first successful launch and mission, carrying a 165 kg (363 lb) dummy payload into orbit as planned. For a moment, Musk and his team rightly basked in the success, and we should not let our present familiarity with spaceflight obscure what Musk and the SpaceX team had accomplished. At this point in history, only massive state-funded space programmes in the USA, Russia and China had succeeded in launching, orbiting and recovering a spacecraft. Now, a private company, run by a man without an aerospace pedigree and funding the majority of the project himself, had accomplished the same. Musk had also been centrally involved in the engineering development of the programme. In fact, he subsequently expressed the view in an interview, with blunt honesty, that he had a part to play in the mission failures as well as the successes:

> And the reason that I ended up being the chief engineer or chief designer, was not because I want to, it's because I couldn't hire anyone. Nobody good would join. So I ended up being that by default. And I messed up the first three launches. The first three launches failed. Fortunately the fourth launch which was – that was the last money that we had for Falcon 1 – the fourth launch worked, or that would have been it for SpaceX.

The fourth launch of Falcon 1 brought tears of jubilation from both Musk and his exceptional team. But the financial problems remained; indeed if anything, they intensified. Both Tesla and SpaceX were literally running out of cash. Now, Musk was faced with one of the hardest decisions of his business career. He explained the quandary in an interview for SXSW in March 2018:

> 2008 was brutal. In 2008 we had the third consecutive failure of the Falcon 1 rocket from SpaceX. Tesla almost went bankrupt. We closed our financing round at 6pm on Christmas Eve 2008. It was the last hour of the last day that it was possible – we would have gone bankrupt two days after Christmas otherwise. And I got divorced. It was like, rough. [. . .] SpaceX is alive by the skin of its teeth, so is Tesla. If things had just gone a little bit the other way

both companies would have been dead. One of the most difficult choices I ever faced was in 2008. I had around 30 to 40 million dollars left in 2008. I had two choices. I could put it all into one company, and then the other company would definitely die, or split it between the two companies. But if I split it between the two companies both might die. When you put your blood, sweat and tears into creating something and building something, it's like a child. So which one? Am I going to let one starve to death? I couldn't bring myself to do it, so I split my money between the two.

Having made his decision, Musk now had to fight for his financial life, scrambling to inject and raise money from whatever sources he could (see the following chapter for further details). Tesla, as indicated, was saved at the last minute, literally hours before the company was to have run out of money. SpaceX also received a last-minute reprieve when, on 23 December 2008, the company was granted NASA's Commercial Resupply Services (CRS) contract, which awarded $1.6 billion to SpaceX to perform 12 cargo transport missions to the International Space Station (ISS), over the period between contract signature and 2016.

Although SpaceX would have to battle financially for many years to come, it had been saved. Furthermore, it had secured exactly the type of major government contract that would act as a proving ground for its capabilities and a stepping stone to yet more commercial work. Musk had proven much in the face of his detractors, demonstrating the tenacity and the commercial intelligence to pull two major companies back from the very edge of failure amidst a devastating economic recession.

THE TRIUMPH OF SPACEX

If we fast-forward the news reel from the end of 2008 to the present day, the change in SpaceX's fortunes could not be greater. In 2018, a decade after the company teetered on the brink, it took an estimated $2 billion in launch revenue – a quarter of the entire global space industry revenue – and was valued at $52 billion. By October 2021, its value had truly reached escape velocity at $100 billion, worth more than aerospace industry leviathan Lockheed Martin. It is today one of the world's largest, most active and most influential space companies. Notably, it remains a private company. Musk has resolutely refused to take the company public, preferring not to cede control of the direction and investments of the company to shareholders. Recounting SpaceX's technical and

Elon Musk's dramatic innovations in space, energy and electric vehicles have earned him access to the highest levels of government interest. Here President Barack Obama gets a guided tour from Musk around the commercial rocket processing facility of SpaceX at Cape Canaveral Air Force Station, Florida, on 15 April 2010.

commercial progress from 2008 to the present in detail would take a book in itself (volumes that do so are given in the Bibliography), but an overview of some key landmarks is useful to orient ourselves to the incredible journey Musk has overseen. Falcon 1, the rocket on which SpaceX was born, made a fifth and final (and successful) launch in July 2009, after which the company's concentration switched to developing Falcon 9, the vehicle that would fulfil NASA's CRS contract. NASA also signed agreements with SpaceX within the Commercial Orbital Transportation Services (COTS) programme, which focused on supporting the development by private companies of vehicles capable of delivering crew and cargo to the ISS. This would be fulfilled by SpaceX's Dragon (aka Dragon 1 and Cargo Dragon), a partially reusable cargo spacecraft that can transport a 6,000 kg (13,300 lb) payload to the ISS or similar future destination, and come back to Earth with 3,000 kg (6,600 lb) of return payload. Dragon had its first successful orbital mission in December 2010 aboard a Falcon 9, and on 22 May 2012 it launched again, this time at the beginning of a nine-day mission to the ISS, with all objectives completed. It was not only the first time a US space vehicle had visited the ISS since the end of the Shuttle programme, it was also the first time a commercial spacecraft had rendezvoused with another spacecraft. Over time, Dragon's capabilities would be extended by Dragon 2, which had two variants: Crew Dragon, capable (according to SpaceX publicity) of taking seven human passengers 'to and from Earth orbit, and beyond', and Cargo Dragon, an improved version of the Dragon 1. Another Dragon milestone was the launch, on 30 May 2020, of Cargo Dragon Demo-2, which took two NASA astronauts (Doug Hurley and Bob Behnken) into orbit and to the

Elon Musk talks with NASA astronaut Bob Behnken during a tour before the launch of the Demo-1 mission, at the Kennedy Space Center, Florida. The Demo-1 mission launched at 2:49am ET on 2 March 2019 and was the first launch of a commercially built and operated American spacecraft and space system designed for humans as part of NASA's Commercial Crew Program.

ISS, in what was another first – the first crewed orbital spaceflight launched from the USA since the final Space Shuttle mission in 2011. Dragon has remained active to this day – as of 9 April 2022, Dragon spacecraft have made 33 total launches and 29 visits to the ISS.

The year 2014 was a significant one for SpaceX commercially and technologically. During that year, SpaceX won nine of the 20 commercial launch contracts open to international competitive bidding. Taking that slice of the pie was a radical shake-up for the global industry. The major French company Arianespace, founded in 1980 and the world's first commercial launch service provider, also won nine, but given the company's long ancestry and established position the fact that it did not win more contracts than SpaceX was an upset in itself. A heavier impact was felt by the US company United Launch Alliance (ULA), founded in 2006 as a joint venture between Lockheed Martin Space and Boeing Defense, Space &

Security, despite the fact that the new company amounted to an effective monopoly over US launch services (something SpaceX challenged legally in 2005, during the formation of ULA). Yet in 2014, ULA won only one contract (for Orbital Sciences' Cygnus space station supply freighter). SpaceX effectively broke the ULA hold over US launches, and the commercial battle between the two continues to this day, with SpaceX in the ascendant. Also in 2014, SpaceX was awarded NASA's Commercial Crew Transportation Capability (CCtCap) contract, to finalize the capability for human transportation to the ISS.

SpaceX has continued to stay at the cutting edge of launch capability, with improvements to existing launch vehicles and the development of new ones. A key operational focus for Musk has been reusability in space launch vehicles to achieve cost efficiencies. Historically, most of the components of rocket launch vehicles, such as main vehicle thrust structures and propellant tanks, have been expendable, one-shot items only. With its Falcon 9 vehicle, SpaceX achieved a partial reusability, the first stage of the rocket returning to Earth and making a visually futuristic controlled vertical landing either at a land-based site or on an autonomous spaceport drone ship (ASDS) barge, essentially a flat-decked ocean-going robotic vessel, providing a safe and stable offshore landing site for the returning rockets. The ASDS in itself is something of a revolution in technology and spaceflight. Musk's naming of the ships – *Just Read the Instructions* (II), *A Shortfall of Gravitas* and *Of Course I Still Love You* – speaks much of his fondness for science fiction, being the same as or similar to spaceships that appear in the *Culture* series of science fiction novels by Iain M. Banks. On 21 December 2021, SpaceX tweeted that 'Falcon 9's first stage has landed on the

Just Read the Instructions droneship, marking the 100th successful landing of an orbital class rocket booster!' – reusability was now an established functional reality of the SpaceX programme.

To ensure that it had full-spectrum payload capabilities, SpaceX also developed the Falcon Heavy. The SpaceX website captures the capability and market separation of this enormous powerplant:

> Falcon Heavy is the most powerful operational rocket in the world by a factor of two. With the ability to lift into orbit nearly 64 metric tons (141,000 lb) Falcon Heavy can lift more than twice the payload of the next closest operational vehicle, the Delta IV Heavy. Falcon Heavy is composed of three Falcon 9 nine-engine cores whose 27 Merlin engines together generate more than 5 million pounds of thrust at liftoff, equal to approximately eighteen 747 aircraft.

Once again, SpaceX was taking a lead in the space game. The Falcon Heavy's maiden flight also had a truly unusual signature, one that speaks volumes about Musk's maverick challenge to traditionalism while also evidencing a strong sense of humour. On 31 March 2017, a Twitter user (cardoso) asked Musk what the test payload would be for the first launch of the Falcon Heavy. Musk cryptically replied: 'Silliest thing we can imagine! Secret payload of 1st Dragon flight was a giant wheel of cheese. Inspired by a friend & Monty Python.' Then on 2 December, Musk finally confirmed the payload in another tweet. It was unexpected, to say the least: 'Payload will be my midnight cherry Tesla Roadster playing Space Oddity. Destination is Mars orbit. Will be in deep space for a billion years or so if it doesn't blow up on ascent.'

In what is arguably the greatest single act in marketing history, Elon Musk's Tesla Roadster glides past Earth, the 'Starman' mannequin wearing a SpaceX space suit in the driving seat. The vehicle was serving as the dummy payload for the February 2018 Falcon Heavy test flight.

FALCON HEAVY AND MARKETING MAGIC

And so it was, on 6 February 2018, the Falcon Heavy lifted off from Kennedy Space Center Launch Complex 39A with Musk's Tesla Roadster mounted on the payload adapter, the second stage of the rocket eventually placing the Roadster in a heliocentric orbit. Compounding the absurdity of the scene, a dummy astronaut, clad in a SpaceX spacesuit, sat with some nonchalance in the driver seat, the left elbow resting on the windowsill, as if the astronaut were out for a casual interstellar Sunday drive. Appropriately, he is called 'Starman', the nod to David's Bowie's music reinforced by 'Space Oddity' and 'Life on Mars' playing on loop from the sound system. The glovebox contains a copy of *The Hitchhiker's Guide to the Galaxy*, also referenced by a sign on the dashboard reading: 'Don't Panic!'

If anything says 'I can do what I want', surely the Roadster in space is the ultimate expression. Cameras aboard the spacecraft transmitted extraordinary pictures (stills and video) showing a Tesla Roadster apparently 'driven' by a spaceman breezing along with the planet Earth as the backdrop. Some might see this as trivializing spaceflight; indeed, firing what essentially amounted to nothing more than automotive junk into space did attract criticism from some scientific and academic quarters. But it was something of a masterpiece of publicity, one that triggered mostly laudatory reflection from the world's marketing media. The title of one piece of analysis: 'There's Advertising and Marketing, and Then There's Elon Musk' (Mark Wnek, *Ad Age*, 8 February 2018) captured the slightly stunned awe of advertisers around the world, humbled before a man who managed to promote two companies at once *in space*, the images of the Roadster achieving media virality with effortless global reach. We will reflect more on Musk as a marketer in the following chapter, but Musk countered his critics with a youthful and optimistic voice that rang a celebratory note: 'Life cannot just be about solving one sad problem after another. There need to be things that inspire you, that make you glad to wake up in the morning and be part of humanity. That is why we did it. We did it for you' (Twitter, 11 March 2018).

At a subsequent Q&A session at the South by Southwest festival (SXSW), Musk deepened the message, explaining that the Tesla space car was no mere stunt, but a tool to encourage humanity to lift its head high once again: 'We really wanted to get the public here to wonder, to get excited about the possibility of something new happening in space – of the space frontier getting pushed forward. The goal of this was to inspire you and make you believe again, just as people believed in the Apollo era, that anything is possible.'

STARLINK AND THE COMMERCIAL RISE OF SPACEX

In January 2015, SpaceX announced the launch of its Starlink satellite internet constellation programme, at the opening of its new development facility in Redmond, Washington. The vision for extending the internet into space appears to have been brewing in Musk's mind since the early 2000s, but according to a *Wall Street Journal* article in November 2014, Musk and tech entrepreneur Grey Wyler were then in discussions about building a constellation of communication satellites called WorldVu, although these did not go further.

Starlink, by contrast, was a visionary ambition to provide global demand for internet broadband capabilities, particularly in those areas of the planet with limited connectivity. While Musk's engineering teams went into action to develop both the satellites and affordable end-user equipment, SpaceX also had to negotiate the numerous regulatory hurdles to deploy the satellites in the first place, with some challenging requirements from the Federal Communications Commission (FCC). For SpaceX's plans were high end – by March 2017, it had filed plans with the FCC to deploy 11,943 satellites in two different low Earth or very low Earth orbits. And this was just the beginning – the plans were eventually to field tens of thousands of Starlink satellites.

On 22 February 2018, two test Starlink satellites – Tintin A and Tintin B – were successfully launched and deployed. On 24 May 2019, 60 'live' satellites were launched, designed to test the network technology. (These achieved some public prominence when filmed from Earth travelling through the night sky, a visible chain of lights in the blackness of space.) On 22 October 2019, Elon Musk was able to tweet the following: 'Sending this tweet through space via Starlink satellite.' Sixty more satellites, this time fully operational variants, went up on 11 November. From this point on, Starlink satellites have been launched with confident regularity, with 2,091 sent up between February 2018 and 2022. As with much of SpaceX's programme, the actual manufacture of the satellites has been kept largely in-house, with SpaceX vice president Jonathan Hofeller stating at the Satellite 2020 conference in Washington, DC, that the company was manufacturing six satellites per day, an astonishing figure that means a significant portion of orbital space will be dominated by SpaceX.

My compact linear narrative of SpaceX's developments since its crisis in 2008 can give the impression of a smooth ascent to ultimate stability and success. In fact, Musk and SpaceX have taken a wild ride, with some major and repeated technical setbacks. Spaceflight, by its very nature, is an ultra-aggressive wrestling match between physics and technology, and SpaceX has not always come out on top. In June 2015, for example, the seventh SpaceX ISS resupply mission, CRS-7, exploded two minutes into flight, and in September 2016 another Falcon 9 was destroyed, this time on the ground in preparation for a static test, in the process obliterating a customer's $200 million communications satellite payload.

But notwithstanding such setbacks, SpaceX has settled into the rhythms of success, and the company attained financial security through a mixture of funding secured and commercial contracts. One of the first major external investments was that

Elon Musk explains the future capabilities of the SpaceX Starship to senior leaders of the North American Aerospace Defense Command, US Northern Command, and Air Force Space Command, 15 April, 2019. Musk's revolutionary economies in spaceflight have attracted the serious attention of government agencies.

made by NASA to support the COTs programme, which awarded $278 million. By mid-2012, following the first SpaceX flights to the ISS, the company's private equity valuation had climbed to $2.4 billion, and in January 2015 the company raised another $1 billion in funding from Google and Fidelity, for 8.33 per cent of the stock. A further $350 million was raised in July 2017, and by the following year the company had performed more than 100 launches with about $12 billion in contract revenue. August 2020 saw another funding round raising $1.9 billion, and another $1.61 billion in February 2021.

It was patently clear investors were recognizing that much of the future of spaceflight might belong to SpaceX and its ambitious leader – by October 2021, the company was valued at $100.3 billion. Of course, the rise of the company's finances was also pushing Musk's personal wealth to ever greater altitudes. According to press data from 2019, Musk holds 54 per cent of the company's equity, with 76 per cent voting rights. Along with the stratospheric growth of Tesla, and the strong performance of some of Musk's other investments and companies, in 2022, he was officially declared the world's richest man, ever, by Forbes (see Chapter 5).

TO THE MOON AND MARS – STARSHIP

The SpaceX journey began with Elon Musk's vision for the 'Mars Oasis'. Although there were subsequent pragmatic redirections to get his fledgling space company established and running, Musk's vision for giving humanity interplanetary options in the future has never waned, and alongside the Falcon 1, Falcon 9 and Crew Dragon programmes there were hints of even greater plans.

During 11–13 November 2005, Musk attended SpaceVision2005, an annual conference for Students for the Exploration and Development of Space (SEDS) at the University of Illinois Urbana-Champaign. There, he began revealing plans for far greater space rocketry than the Falcon 1 that was due to launch just weeks later. Musk also outlined plans to build more powerful engine types than the Merlin 1 type then in use on Falcons 1, 5 and 9. A perceptive audience member asked Musk about a particularly large test stand at the Texas engine facility, which SpaceX called the 'BFTS', noting that its scale implied it could take nearly five times the thrust of a Falcon 9 first stage. In response, Musk described his vision for a 'Merlin 2', a monster engine capable of lifting the heaviest of payloads. Multiple Merlin 2s, he told the conference, would be used to develop what he wryly called the 'BFR' – the 'B' stands for 'Big' and the 'R' stands for Rocket. (With this information, it is also easy to work out what 'BFTS' stands for.) Musk argued the long-term focus for Merlin 2 development – Moon and Mars exploration – although he admitted that 'We're not quite sure how to pay for that vehicle.'

But while the idea for the BFR was initially sketchy, it steadily acquired sharper lines both in Musk's mind and on the developmental drawing board. In 2007, Musk gave an interview for *Wired* magazine. The subsequent article by Carl Hoffman, published on 22 May, tellingly carried the title 'Elon Musk Is Betting His Fortune on a Mission Beyond Earth's Orbit'. In the interview, Musk responded to an argument by John Pike, a space analyst at GlobalSecurity.org, who challenged Musk's belief that he could change the fundamental financial equation of putting payloads into low Earth orbit, about $10,000 per pound in weight. Musk responded with ebullient defiance: 'But I want to make rockets 100 times, if not 1,000 times, better. The ultimate objective is to make humanity a multiplanet species. Thirty years from now, there'll be a base on the moon and on Mars, and people will be going back and forth on SpaceX rockets.'

More hints and details about just how Musk was going to tackle these challenges trickled out over subsequent years, given extra credence by the fact that SpaceX was becoming a respected aerospace company. Musk himself was by the 2010s regarded as a serious space engineer who was raising the pulse and possibilities of spaceflight, while at the same time reducing its costs. Then in September 2016, Musk made a lengthy SpaceX presentation entitled 'Making Humans a Multiplanetary Species'. The title promised substantial revelations, and the audience wouldn't be disappointed.

Musk opened the presentation with a simple question: 'So how do we figure out how to take you to Mars and create a self-sustaining city, a city that is not merely an outpost but it [sic] could become a planet in its own right? Thus we could become a truly multi-planet species.' Working through his set of presentation slides, he next made a scientific case for Mars as the prime objective for space colonization, comparing it to the properties of Earth in a comparative table. (In the final row of the table – 'People' – the slide gave the figure '7 billion' for Earth and '0' for Mars – one senses that the Mars figure was given to show potentiality for settlement, not resignation to realities.)

After this, Musk moved on to the economics of Mars settlement. Given that historical spaceflight had been inordinately expensive, this was an important moment in the presentation. How could he do it without burning up entire fortunes? Musk explained that using Apollo-era technology, travel to Mars would indeed be prohibitively expensive at every level, costing about $10 billion per person. At such prices, significant population transfers from Earth to Mars were simply out of the question. Musk then shifted the conceptual framework profoundly. Instead, he argued, he wanted to reduce the per-person cost of going to Mars to about the median price of a house in the USA, about $200,000. Only then could Mars colonization become a genuine off-planet possibility, the decision to move to Mars carrying similar decision-making weight to moving home or having a major change in career.

Given the sheer disparity between the $10 billion and $200,000 cost models, clearly some proof was in order – Musk was arguing for a 5 million per cent improvement in the cost per ton to Mars. Slide 13 of the deck therefore listed the four key technological developments that had to occur to achieve this goal:

1. Full reusability
2. Refilling in orbit
3. Propellant production on Mars
4. Right propellant

Any accusations that Musk might have been on a flight of fancy were dispelled in the subsequent section of the presentation, in which he explained the physics, developed theory and the technologies behind achieving each of the bullet points.

The presentation eventually built up to the moment to reveal the 'System Architecture' – the actual details of how the Mars missions would be performed and the types of craft that would make the epic multi-month journeys to the red planet. Simplifying somewhat here, the Mars spacecraft would launch from Earth, a huge booster rocket taking the craft into space. (The booster would, after separation, return to Earth and make a controlled and autonomous landing, thereafter being reused for subsequent launches.) At the beginning of its journey into space, the spaceship would rendezvous with tanker ships, performing an in-flight refuelling in the vacuum of space. (In an earlier stage of the presentation, Musk explained that 'Not refilling in orbit would require a 3-stage vehicle at 5–10× the size and cost', and also that 'Spreading the required lift capability across multiple launches substantially reduces development costs and compresses schedules.) The tankers then return to Earth while the Mars vehicle now begins its journey to Mars – this epic haul across space would take some seven to nine months, traversing about 480 million km (300 million miles). The spacecraft would eventually make a vertical landing on Mars and offload its passengers and payload. Propellant for the return journey would be manufactured on the planet, the production utilizing materials mined from Mars itself. (Musk explained in the slides that 'Bringing return propellant requires approximately 5 times as much mass departing Earth.') When the time is right, the spacecraft then makes the return journey to Earth, being turned around quickly for its next flight. The overall vision for reusability is 1,000 uses per booster, 100 per tanker and 12 per ship.

The detail of Musk's Mars ambitions goes to the heart of his engineering method, and not least the reasoning from 'first principles' outlined in detail in Chapter 6. At the beginning of the presentation, Musk showed some numinous pictures of Mars and spoke in reverent tones about the possibility that one day we might just live there. At that point in the proceedings, it almost had the ring of implausible 1950s visions of intergalactic travel, more akin to *Star Trek* than SpaceX. Less than halfway through the presentation, however, Musk has transitioned to an eminently believable prospect, one that possibly can be timetabled into the near future. For Musk, if the logic of the core principles and technologies is sound in the smallest increments, then scaling up to a grandiose scale is equally logical. His ultimate vision does indeed stray into the realms of sci-fi, explicitly so:

> Over time there would be many spaceships – we would ultimately have over a thousand or more spaceships waiting in orbit. So the Mars Colonial Fleet would depart en masse, kind of like *Battlestar Galactica* [. . .] But it actually makes sense to load the spaceships into orbit, because you have two years to do so [the rendezvous orbit for going to Mars comes around every 26 months].

An appreciative round of applause came from the audience when Musk finally revealed the instrument of his ambitions, at this stage in its evolution simply referred to as the 'Mars Vehicle'. The graphics showed a monster piece of kit, the combined booster and ship standing to a height of 122 m (400 ft), even taller than the Saturn V that performed the Apollo missions, at 111 m (364 ft). Every statistic about the vehicle represented a leap beyond historical parameters – a 10,500-tonne lift-off mass (Saturn V – 3,039 tonnes); a 13,033-tonne lift-off thrust (Saturn V – 3,579 tonnes); an expendable low Earth orbit payload of 550 tonnes (Saturn V – 135 tonnes). Clearly, the Mars Vehicle was intended to be a spacecraft that represented the next stage in the evolution of space exploration. Musk reflected on its design, but also made clear that this was just the first step up the evolutionary ladder:

> It's quite big. The funny thing is that in the long term the ships will be even bigger than this. This will be relatively small compared to the Mars interplanetary ships of the future. But it kind of needs to be about this size because in order to fit about one hundred people in the pressurized section and carry the luggage; and all of the unpressurized cargo, to build propellant plants, and build everything from iron foundries to pizza joints, you name it, we need to carry a lot of cargo.

The Mars Vehicle would eventually acquire a fitting name – Starship. During the 2015 presentation, the slide deck offered a Gantt chart revealing the projected timelines of the mission to Mars. With the major technologies developed by 2019, booster and orbital testing would take place from 2019 to late 2022, and Mars flights themselves would start in the later months of 2022. In reality, these schedules have had to move somewhat. Practical Starship development began in 2019 in Florida and Texas and was accompanied by a stinging commercial decision. In January that year, SpaceX announced that it would be compelled to lay off 10 per cent of its 6,000-strong workforce in order to make the financials work for development of Starlink and Starship combined. The company press release stated: 'To continue delivering for our customers and to succeed in developing interplanetary spacecraft and a global space-based Internet, SpaceX must become a leaner company. Either of these developments, even when attempted separately, have bankrupted other organizations. This means we must part ways with some talented and hardworking members of our team.' The pursuit of Starship would have other significant knock-on effects. In March 2022, for example, SpaceX announced that it was to end production of its Crew Dragon spacecraft, instead focusing future efforts on completing development of Starship.

Starship is perhaps the apogee of Musk's space programme, in his lifetime. The SpaceX website proudly declares of the ship: 'SpaceX's Starship spacecraft and Super Heavy rocket (collectively referred to as Starship) represent a fully reusable transportation system designed to carry both crew and cargo to Earth orbit, the Moon, Mars and beyond. Starship will be the world's most powerful launch vehicle ever developed, with the ability to carry in excess of 100 metric tonnes to Earth orbit.' The specifications of Starship have changed since the visions of 2015, but only marginally so,

Despite SpaceX's success, the road to space has not always been an easy one for Musk. Here he surveys the remnants of Starship SN8, after it exploded on landing in December 2020 in Boca Chica, Texas.

and it remains the most powerful rocket ever to lift off from Earth, with the highest payload capacity. Since 2019, the programme has evolved from a series of static or short hops to sub-orbital launches, several of the prototypes being destroyed in the fiery process. But on 5 May 2021, Starship SN15 successfully completed the first high-altitude test from the Starbase centre in Texas. Starship is not just about Mars. In April 2021, NASA announced that it had selected SpaceX and its Starship 'to continue development of the first commercial human lander that will safely carry the next two American astronauts to the lunar surface', as part of its Artemis programme. Where Starship and Musk will go in the more distant future remains to be seen.

CHAPTER 4
TESLA AND THE TWITTERVERSE

Electric vehicles (EVs) are not new. Far from it. In fact, EVs are almost as old as the invention of electrical supply and automobiles. Concepts for the development of battery-powered EVs first emerge in the early years of the 19th century. Somewhere between 1832 and 1839, British inventor Robert Anderson put together a three-wheeled 'electric carriage' which, powered by a disposable lead battery, could trundle along at a sedate but workable 12 km/h (7.5 mph). It was in the second half of the century, however, that EVs started to appear regularly and in significant numbers. In 1881, Frenchman Gustave Trouvé unveiled his Trouvé Tricycle, another three-wheeled EV powered by two engines working off several interconnected lead batteries, giving it a top speed of 18 km/h (11 mph) and a range of up to 26 km (16 miles). In Germany, the Maschinenfabrik A. Flocken company in Coburg produced, from 1888, the four-wheeled Flocken Elektrowagen, regarded by many as the first true electric car. In 1898, the Belgian EV *La Jamais Contente,* essentially a four-wheeled metal torpedo with a prominently perched driver, reached a speed of 105.882 km/h (65.792 mph), for a short time holding the world land speed record.

EVs debuted in the USA in the late 1880s and early 1890s courtesy of Scottish-born chemist and inventor William Morrison. His work on developing more effective storage batteries led to a self-propelled electrical carriage demonstrator fitted with 24 of his batteries; the vehicle was capable of carrying up to 12 passengers and had a maximum speed of 32 km/h (20 mph). Only 12 of these vehicles were made, but the idea was persuasive. By 1900, 38 per cent of all motor vehicles in the USA were electric (compared to 40 per cent steam and 22 per cent gasoline). New York City even had a fleet of 60 electric taxis. Even the likes of Porsche and Henry Ford would either develop or investigate EVs.

In many ways, EVs of the early 20th century were superior to the emerging types powered by the internal combustion engine. But as history now knows, the internal combustion engine won out. From Henry Ford's introduction of the mass-produced Model T in 1908, and with the global expansion of oil extraction, petrol-powered vehicles offered the masses more affordable, convenient and accessible vehicles – by the 2000s, there would be more than a billion such vehicles on the planet.

Yet the pendulum began to swing ever so slightly back from the 1960s and 1970s. Global oil crises, precipitated by conflict in the major oil-producing states of the Middle East, compelled the world to look hard at its vehicular dependence on fossil fuels, and to reinvestigate the possibilities of EVs. General Motors (GM) and American Motor Company (AMC) both produced either prototype or small-scale production EVs during the 1970s, although the core challenge of EVs – limited range – meant that the vehicles remained little more than a thought trial. In the 1980s and 1990s, however, increasing environmental awareness at government level, accompanied by energy and clean air legislation in some countries (including the USA), reconnected the idea of EVs to the engineering grid. GM designed and developed the EV1 and manufactured it between 1996 and 1999. It had a range of 128 km (80 miles) and acceleration of 0–80 km/h (0–50 mph) in just seven seconds (EVs are capable of delivering more torque than gas-powered cars, hence they often have exceptional acceleration). Battery technologies were also improving. In 1997, Japan's Toyota company released the hybrid electric Prius, powered from a nickel metal hydride battery. Unlike the short-lived EV1 – the world's first mass-produced EV – the Prius went on to roaring success: by 2017, more than 6.1 million had been sold. But by this time, there was a powerful new player in the EV market. This competing company would become, by 2022, the true giant of EVs, with a market capitalization of more than $1 trillion and holding 23 per cent of the battery EV market globally, positioned as the leading EV seller by significant margins, even compared against the world's biggest carmakers. Founded only in 2003, the company is Tesla, guided by its CEO Elon Musk.

MUSK AND THE EV MISSION

EVs reflect two central foci within Musk's worldview – energy and environmentalism. Musk's fascination with innovation in electrical energy has deep roots – remember his absorption in all matters ultracapacitors during his youth – and this intellectual interest has connected with rising concern about Earth's environmental fragility, converting a topic of study into a world-beating company.

Musk is certainly not a climate-change-denying industrialist. In numerous speeches and writings, he strongly backs the scientific arguments for man-made climate change, which he sees as a threat if not to humanity as a whole, then at least to the way of life of hundreds of millions of citizens on Earth (especially the 40 per cent of the human population who live on or near a coastline, places most vulnerable to rising sea levels). Fossil fuels lie at the heart of the problem:

> I mean, there's definitely, there are many important issues in the world. This is not the only important issue, but it is I think, the thing that will have the biggest negative effect on humanity, if we do not address it. In general terms, what is needed to address the climate crisis, and this is the thing that if we do, what actions can we take that will accelerate the transition out of the fossil fuel era?

Musk may have built one of the world's biggest car companies, but he is clear-sighted about the link between the consumption of fossil fuels and the decline in our atmosphere. His interest in EVs, therefore, has parallels with his pursuit of space exploration – the technological advancement of both is not just a matter of engineering curiosity or entrepreneurial pursuit, but rather critical parts of the human future. Musk intends to be at the cutting edge of both.

With a bit less gravity, however, Musk is interested in electric cars perhaps because another option for solving the fossil fuel crisis – taking people out of their individual vehicles and putting them on public transport systems – is a policy that doesn't exactly fill Musk with enthusiasm. With tongue firmly in cheek, he expressed his views on public transport at a Tesla event running alongside a Neural Information Processing Systems Conference in Long Beach, California, in December 2017:

> I think public transport is painful. It sucks. Why do you want to get on something with a lot of other people, that doesn't leave

where you want it to leave, doesn't start where you want it to start, doesn't end where you want it to end? And it doesn't go all the time. [...] It's a pain in the ass. That's why everyone doesn't like it. And there's like a bunch of random strangers, one of who might be a serial killer, OK, great. And so that's why people like individualized transport, that goes where you want, when you want.

So public transport is out. Instead, Musk has focused on three primary routes out of the fossil-fuel-induced crisis, all of which he has engaged with commercially: battery energy storage, solar power and EVs. All of these enterprises have been exercised under the Tesla Inc. brand, but in this chapter, we will focus principally on Tesla as a carmaker – the following chapter will delve into solar power, alternative energy, AI and some of Musk's many other important pursuits.

As we have seen from the quick stats at the beginning of this chapter, Tesla has upended the world of carmaking and selling. In many ways it is *the* face of EVs, albeit one in an increasingly competitive market. Like most of Musk's enterprises, it began as a disruptive idea, executed by small groups of people in workshops. The very earliest roots of Tesla were not sown by Musk himself, at least not practically, but it is impossible to argue that the giant EV producer that exists today would not exist in the form it does were it not for his investment, ideas, engineering compulsions and commercial vision. The relationship between the man and company is an intimate one, not least in the public's eyes. Thus, in this chapter we will also explore how Musk relates to the worlds of advertising and social media, all of which have been crucial in the historical growth of Tesla. In these areas also, Musk has shaken up the way things are done. As a quick point to illustrate this: Tesla spends $0 on direct advertising, while other carmakers often spend hundreds of millions. Why and how this is so, we will explore, but for sure, Musk is a game-changer, making his fair share of friends and enemies along the way.

THE FOUNDATIONS

In total, five people are legally regarded as the co-founders of Tesla. They are Martin Eberhard, Marc Tarpenning, Ian Wright, J.B. Straubel and Elon Musk. The list has not just evolved by common agreement. In fact, in June 2009, Eberhard – once the Tesla CEO, but subsequently removed from the position – filed a lawsuit alleging that Musk had attempted to 'rewrite history' and effectively remove him from both the company and its origin story. Musk pushed back with a vigorous countersuit. The Tesla response, issued by company spokesperson Rachel Konrad, was uncompromising:

> This lawsuit is an unfair personal attack and, more importantly, paints an inaccurate picture of Tesla's history. This lawsuit is a fictionalized account of Tesla's early years—it's twisted and wrong, and we welcome the opportunity to set the record straight. As the media have already covered exhaustively, Tesla's full board of directors unanimously fired Martin shortly after discovering that the cost of the car was more than twice what Martin portrayed it to be at the time. Incidentally, Tesla will likely be filing counterclaims and in the process present an accurate account of the company's history.

But in September 2009 the list of co-founders was legally agreed on the five names opposite. Clearly, the foundation of Tesla has been a matter of some complexity, and acrimony.

Tesla was born out of the gradual alignment of several stars. Musk's first practical intersection with EVs was a meeting with a man called J.B. Straubel. Straubel was Musk's kind of guy. He was a lifelong engineer and have-a-go inventor, but with serious intellectual heft – he went on to graduate from Stanford in energy systems and engineering (a major that he essentially developed himself). Straubel was especially focused on the possibilities of developing clean-energy vehicles, even turning a beaten-up old Porsche into an EV that, for a time, held the world record for EV acceleration, then adding hybrid functionality to extend the car's range. While at Stanford, he also laboured with a like-minded group of enthusiasts on solar-powered vehicles and following graduation, he developed some of the world's first gas-turbine/electric hybrid vehicles for a company called Rosen Motors, led by engineer Harold Rosen (the inventor of the geostationary satellite), and on developing an all-electric aircraft, also in partnership with Rosen.

In the early 2000s, Straubel was particularly fascinated by the possibilities of using lithium ion (li-ion) batteries, a power source with many advantages over traditional battery types, including a high energy density, a lower self-discharge rate, lower maintenance requirements, higher cell voltages and greater versatility of application. Rechargeable li-ion batteries had established themselves in the electronics industry during the 1990s, but Straubel and his solar-team friends from university began doing the maths on how thousands of li-ion batteries could be connected together to provide sufficient power to drive a vehicle. Straubel created a design concept, but just needed someone to invest $100,000 to help him actually build it.

Here, Musk enters the picture. Straubel was introduced to Musk by Rosen, and over lunch, Musk bought into the possibilities of li-ion EVs and agreed to invest $10,000. Straubel also introduced Musk to a Los Angeles-based company called AC Propulsion, founded in 1992 to develop EV technology (especially alternating-current-based drivetrain systems) and to provide engineering support to automotive companies. The company had developed prototypes of a sports car EV called the tzero, which included innovations such as regenerative braking and had a dramatic 0–60 mph (0–97 km/h) time of 4.07 seconds. They were also working on a far less flamboyant five-door hatchback EV called the eBox. Musk was allowed to take the tzero for a spin, loved it and wanted to invest in taking the vehicle to market, but the offer went nowhere. What it did, however, was galvanize Musk's interest in building his own EV.

At the same time as all this was occurring, two California-based engineers were also working on their own development of a li-ion vehicle. They were Martin Eberhard and Marc Tarpenning. Both men were electrical engineers and natural entrepreneurs, and by the time they turned their thoughts to EVs they had already achieved high success in joint ventures. Together, they had founded NuvoMedia in 1996, through which they developed the world's first e-reader, known as the Rocket eBook. Although the Rocket eBook would not survive long into the 2000s, NuvoMedia itself was bought in 2000 by Gemstar–TV Guide International for $187 million. So, the pair of entrepreneurs now had money to invest in other projects.

Like Musk, Eberhard also had a go at turning AC Propulsion into the model of where he wanted to go with electric vehicles, but when that didn't work out, they decided to form their own company. It was founded on 1 July 2003, the name of the company inspired by the legendary Serbian American engineer and inventor. It was called Tesla Motors.

THE INDUSTRY

Before we march on with the Tesla narrative, some context is required both to understand the obstacles Tesla would face as an automotive start-up and to appreciate what Musk and his team have done with the company and its products to date. For generations, most of the vehicle marques we see around us have been predictably familiar – Ford, BMW, Toyota, GM, Jaguar and so on. The principal reason for this limited batch of car manufacturers is that the financial and production barriers to enter the market are so extreme, if you want to be more than a small bespoke car builder. The industry costs associated with the development of a new car, from initial concept, through R&D, prototype construction, testing and eventually arriving at the production design, commonly range between $1 billion and $6 billion, depending on the level of innovation or re-use from previous vehicles. The development process involves hundreds of engineers, working at costly and often exclusive facilities, with massive fixed costs. Then there is the matter of manufacturing, involving vast production plants, thousands of factory-floor employees, armies of robots, thousands of tons of raw materials, hundreds of thousands of components, plus shipping from distant destinations. Once a car rolls off production, it also has to be sold at a profit, in a brutally competitive market deeply subject to the vagaries of major economic shifts. Profit margins for new cars vary profoundly according to the manufacturer and prevailing market conditions but tend to be in the 10–20 per cent range, although the net profit of major carmakers all told is typically single digits, or a loss.

The message appears simple – if you want to enter the automotive business, you ideally need billions in the bank, a huge engineering and manufacturing infrastructure, and a compelling product. Even scale has been no protection – many of the world's largest carmakers have slid into bankruptcy proceedings, some emerging from the other side in revamped form but many not surviving. But Musk sees things differently. In a tweet in March 2021, he made a deep claim: 'Tesla & Ford are the only American carmakers not to have gone bankrupt out of 1000s of car startups. Prototypes are easy, production is hard & being cash flow positive is excruciating.' Based on his experience of Tesla, he was right on every count.

FROM INVESTOR TO CEO

Given the towering walls blocking mass car manufacture, Eberhard and Tarpenning's ambition for Tesla was focused on developing a vehicle for the upper end of the market, targeting affluent individuals who had embraced the eco future, and who wanted a sports car that expressed both their fashionably rich status and their environmental credentials. It was a canny positioning and one that Musk would eventually continue. In terms of a future cascade to more mass-produced vehicles, the initial car would hopefully provide the seed money to introduce new models at greater economies of scale.

As wealthy as they were, Eberhard and Tarpenning did not have the R&D resources to develop a brand-new car from scratch, so they were on the scout for ways to streamline the process. The initial plan was to license the powerplant technology developed by AC Propulsion and marry it to the chassis of the elegant Lotus Elise (the chassis would have to be stretched by 127 mm/5 in to accommodate the EV components). Then, instead of selling the car through dealerships, they would instead create a publicity buzz around the vehicle and sell direct to the customer. The plan was savvy, but even though they were looking to bypass swathes of traditional development costs, building a prototype was still going to be an expensive process. They needed investors.

Elon Musk now re-entered the stage in earnest. The three men met in LA to discuss the proposition and Musk bought into the plan. He invested $6.5 million in creating the Tesla EV. The size of the investment made Musk the largest shareholder in the company, and gave him the position of company chairman, two factors that might have seemed secondary at the time, but which would become of signal importance later on.

For now, the men set to work building a car company. A team of talented engineers was brought together and a workshop facility bought and set up in San Carlos, San Mateo County, California. Musk quickly drew Straubel into the company, tasking him with developing the truly critical component of this vehicle – the battery storage pack. We must remember that li-ion EV powerplants were still in their experimental infancy at this stage; Straubel and those who helped him would be at the genuine cutting edge of clean-energy technology. There was much riding on their talents and innovations.

Despite an extremely basic workshop, certainly in comparison to those of the large carmakers, and a team of just 18 people, Tesla pulled off the incredible feat of designing a working prototype between October 2004 and January 2005, due in part to their light and quick management processes. The new car would be called the Roadster. Musk, having taken the vehicle for a test drive, was encouraged both by the product and the progress and put an additional $9 million of his own money into the car. In 2006–07, furthermore, Musk pulled in $105 million from tech-hungry venture capitalists and investors, wanting an early slice of the cake. They included Valor Equity Partners, Draper Fisher Jurvetson, Google co-founders Sergey Brin and Larry Page, Compass Technology Partners and former eBay president Jeff Skoll.

Arrival at prototype stage, however, still left a long, winding and arduous road ahead. There were endless engineering challenges with the new technology, such as how to control heat build-up and how to prevent fires in thousands of individual but connected batteries (the final production Roadster would contain 6,831 batteries in each unit). The total weight of the battery was about 454 kg (1,000 lb). Another significant change was that it was decided to move away from the Elise body and create something far more bespoke to the Tesla brand, made out of carbon fibre. Looking back through early Tesla press content, Tesla was keen to break the widespread idea that the production Roadster was nothing more than an electrified Elise. In a two-part 'Mythbusters' blog in March 2008, Darryl Siry, the vice president of sales, marketing and service at the company, acknowledged that 'One of the more common misconceptions about the Tesla Roadster is that it is an electrified Lotus Elise.' He went on to explain that the Tesla actually had only a 7 per cent parts share with the Elise:

> So you could say that the Tesla is similar to a Lotus Elise, except it has a totally different drivetrain, body panels, aluminum tub, rear sub-frame, brakes, ABS system, HVAC and rear suspension. The Tesla also neglects to carry over the gas tank, emissions equipment and exhaust. If you were to try to convert an Elise to a Tesla and started throwing away parts that aren't carried over what you would basically be left with a windshield, dashboard (complete with airbags!), front wishbones and a removable soft top.

By now, Musk himself was heavily involved in the design process of the new car, making regular contributions to the features and layout of the vehicle. He was also getting the publicity machine into full swing, creating a crackle of excitement about the vehicle that was about to hit the scene, a previously improbable fusion of Silicon Valley know-how, conspicuous consumption, high-end performance and environmental awareness.

The car had its initial unveiling to the public on 19 July 2006, at an invitation-only event in an aircraft hangar at Santa Monica Airport. Some 350 celebrities, business leaders and media movers and shakers attended to see the second Roadster prototype, EP2, on display. The technical issues the engineering teams were still wrestling with were not up for discussion. Instead, the audience was presented with a $90,000 car with a 0–60 mph of 4 seconds, a range of 400 km (250 miles) per charge, and all the bells-and-whistles features one would expect of a supercar. Musk pumped up the product, emphasizing that 'Until today, all electric cars have sucked.'

Pre-orders flooded in, and the media were getting excited. But back in the workshop, all was not well, at a serious scale. Tesla was undoubtedly a company challenging the traditional routes of developing and building a car. It found maverick ways to bypass some of the stinging costs of R&D; for example, instead of taking the Roadster prototypes to a high-cost industry facility for sub-zero testing, they simply bought and converted a freezer lorry. But the problems and the associated delays mounted as they attempted to take the Roadster into production and full launch. There were serious technical issues with the transmission, which was found to be failing at a mean average of about 3,200 km (2,000 miles). A battery production plant being built in Thailand was, at least initially, disastrously unfit for purpose. There was a complex international production system, with body panels made in France, power units in Taiwan, battery packs in Thailand (the parts having been shipped in from China) then shipped to England, with Lotus assembling the body of the car and installing the battery packs in the UK, after which the Roadsters eventually shipped to the USA (Vance 2015: 173). Things were starting to get out of control, especially as investors' money was being spent at an alarming rate.

There were also tensions at the top. According to Vance, Tarpenning said Musk was 'livid' when a *New York Times* profile of Tesla focused more on Eberhard and the car than they did on Tesla's biggest shareholder (Vance 2015: 167–68). Matters were made worse by what Eberhard allegedly saw as Musk's frequent interference with vehicle design.

Eventually, matters reached a peak. Valor Equity sent its astute and experienced managing director of operations, Tim Watkins, to analyse what was happening at Tesla. He came away with a dreadful picture of mounting chaos, the problems including runaway costs, poor financial management, failures in vehicle functionality and major supplier issues. By his calculations, Tesla would actually lose about $115,000 per vehicle (Vance 2015: 175). Once Watkins made his report to Musk and the board, there was a move to make a change at the top. In August 2007, Eberhard lost his position as CEO (to be fair, according to Vance, Eberhard had been asking for this anyway) and instead became president of technology (Tarpenning was vice president of electrical engineering). Board member and manufacturing logistics expert Michael Marks temporarily stepped into the CEO role and sought to bring more organizational order to Tesla production. In December 2007, Marks was replaced by entrepreneur Ze'ev Drori. Notably, both Eberhard and Tarpenning left Tesla altogether in January 2008, and on decidedly poor terms with Musk. The following October, Musk himself stepped up and because the Tesla CEO.

In 2008, as we saw in the previous chapter, the world seemed to decide to stack itself up against Elon Musk. Energized by Musk's aggressive and involved style of management, Tesla managed to put the Roadster into production. At the same time, another vehicle, known provisionally as the 'Whitestar', was under development. This would become the Model S, a five-door sedan aimed at widening Tesla's market from upper-end sporting luxury to mid-range family car. The Model S, as it turned out, would be both the salvation and the making of Tesla, but that was some way in the future. Back in 2008, Tesla was haemorrhaging about $100,000 per day and even though more than a thousand Roadsters had been reserved, production and quality issues meant that only 50 had been delivered. Press scepticism about the upstart company was mounting.

Above all, Musk needed money to survive, as the coffers began to run dry. Bankruptcy soon looked like likely, not an outside possibility. Musk's round-the-clock efforts to save his companies are now the stuff of legend. He went to every source he could find – investors, employees, friends. He put in his own money and sold quantities of his shares in SolarCity (see the following chapter for more about this company). A lifeline was thrown when one of Musk's own investments, Everdream (a company that provided remote office and data services, founded by Musk's cousins – see Chapter 5) was bought by Dell computers in a $340 million acquisition, which gave Musk a sudden $15 million windfall to plough straight back into Tesla. SpaceX provided Tesla with loans, although as we saw in the previous chapter, the financial struggles to enter the space race were also exacting a cost on Musk's finances. But it was still not enough, and as Christmas 2008 approached, Musk had just weeks of payroll funds left.

Arguably the worst moment of a terrible year came in early December, when a deal for VantagePoint Capital Partners to match the $20 million Musk himself had raised suddenly hit a block, as the investors questioned the valuation of Tesla. According to Vance, Musk began to suspect that the venture capital firm was attempting to make manoeuvres to take ultimate control of Tesla, and possibly sell it off to one of the big carmakers. Under intense pressure, Musk held his nerve, even claiming that he would fund Tesla himself from another SpaceX loan. On Christmas Eve, literally a matter of hours before Tesla would have folded, Musk won the staring contest, and the funding came through.

For now, Tesla was still a going concern. It was far from out of the woods, not least because there remained many technical issues with the Roadster, which Tesla was spending time and money to resolve – in 2004, Tesla had estimated that the Roadster would cost $25 million to develop; by 2008, it had actually cost $140 million (although that was still way below anything that could be achieved by the wider automotive industry). Musk drove his team on unrelentingly, and was ever making demands on cost, schedules and quality that, to many, seemed like impossibilities. It has been noted by some of Musk's executives, however, that a person who said something was impossible would often be fired, then Musk would take over the job personally and deliver exactly what his employee had claimed was undoable.

And then, the sales began to mount. By the scale of the big carmakers, the Tesla sales figures were not huge by any score – 147 cars went out in January 2009, and 2,500 between 2008 and 2012. But remember that these were years of global financial crisis, when hundreds of companies were going to the wall and hundreds of thousands losing their jobs. Tesla was not only surviving, but in its way was showing signs that it might be able to thrive, and with a ground-breaking new product. The company again became hot property for investors.

THE BREAKTHROUGH

The Roadster would not, however, be Tesla's breakthrough car, not least because Roadster production ceased in January 2012. It would make way for the second of Tesla's offerings, launched six months later – the Model S.

The Model S was an evolutionary next step for Tesla. It was still a luxury vehicle, but instead of a sports car it was to be a high-quality five-door sedan sold around the $50,000–$70,000 mark, but again with all the performance, economy and environmental advantages of a Tesla EV, plus a range of hi-tech features that would make the vehicle a compelling proposition. The path to production was paved with complications, obstacles and battles. Getting the design and functionality to Musk's bar-raising specifications was a profound challenge for his team. In terms of the overall look, the task was originally handed to Danish-American automotive designer and entrepreneur Henrik Fisker, who had previously worked for BMW, Ford and Aston Martin, as well as running his own engineering company, Fisker Coachbuild. His initial designs were not received well and were regarded by many in the company as uninspiring. Then, in 2007, Fisker left to establish his own design company, Fisker Automotive, and in 2008, unveiled the Fisker Karma, a hybrid luxury sports car (later all-electric) of outstanding beauty. This led to Tesla filing a lawsuit against Fisker, saying he had stolen design ideas while working under Tesla's coin, although Fisker ultimately won the case against him.

In Fisker's place came Franz von Holzhausen, previously of Volvo, GM and Mazda, a talented man looking to find creative liberty away from the corporate layers of the big carmakers. Operating out of a workshop placed within the SpaceX factory, von Holzhausen and a small team of engineers created the layout and look of the Model S in about three months flat. But Musk was never far away and his scrutiny was laser-like.

There is much of Musk in the Model S. Every contour, every button, every device, every feature – nothing escaped his view. After each minor round of improvements, he would view or drive the vehicle and come back with a long list of improvements, reportedly logged in his memory rather than on paper. He would reel off the required amendments to his subordinates, and when the car was presented back to him following further work, Musk would remember each item of concern and note whether it was resolved to his satisfaction. Innovation oozed out of the vehicle, exterior and interior. Instead of the typical car dashboard, it would feature only a large 43 cm (17 in) central touch screen computer, fully internet enabled – a feature that had never before been tested or installed for vehicular use. The door handles retracted when not in use. One of the biggest innovations was the body, which Musk decided should be made out of aluminium rather than steel, thereby offering a considerable weight saving (increasing car and battery performance), but far harder to work into a car body.

After a protracted period of exhaustive refining, the Model S was finally unveiled in March 2009. Packed with ground-breaking technology and unheard-of service support (see below), the new car seized the attention not only of the media, which gave ebullient feedback, but now also of the big carmakers, many of which had been treating Tesla with patronizing dismissal. Some embraced Tesla's innovation, particularly Daimler AG (owner of the Mercedes-Benz brand), which acquired a 10 per cent stake in Tesla for a $50 million investment. Tesla would go on to develop battery pack and charger technologies for Daimler vehicles (note that Tesla had used the Mercedes CLS as a baseline in their development of the Model S), but Tesla still faced the problem of how to build the vehicle in sufficient volume. In short, it needed a factory and all the kit that went in it, but that was going to cost huge money.

Two breakthroughs solved the problem. First, Tesla, particularly through the efforts of Diarmuid O'Connell, the supremely capable vice president of business development, managed to secure in June

2009 a $465 million loan from the US Department of Energy, part of the $8 billion Advanced Technology Vehicles Manufacturing Loan Program. The money was intended to help build a new factory, but another fortuitous opportunity arose. A giant car assembly plant in Fremont, California, constructed in the 1980s as a joint venture between GM and Toyota, suddenly came on the market as GM filed for bankruptcy the same month that Tesla won the government loan. A large part of the plant, which included all the build technologies and had 5,000 unemployed workers to draw on, was bought by Tesla for just $42 million, and Toyota took a 2.5 per cent stake in Tesla for a $50 million investment.

All the pieces of the jigsaw were falling into place, but further fundraising was required to give the Model S the best chance possible. On 29 June 2010, therefore, Tesla became a public company with an IPO on NASDAQ; it was the first time that a US carmaker had issued an IPO since Ford in 1956. Despite some negative press analysis before the IPO, based on the heavy losses and costs Tesla had incurred over previous years, the IPO was a resounding success, issuing 13.3 million shares at $17 a share and raising $226 million. The share price would increase 41 per cent by the following day and by the following July it had hit an astonishing $130.

The Model S has become one the great automotive success stories in modern history. The latest battery pack features some 7,920 battery cells and depending on the model, can deliver a range of between 401 km (249 miles) and 647 km (402 miles) on a single charge. The battery itself is at the cutting edge of electrical storage with the addition of silicon (alongside conventional graphite) in the anode, increasing the energy density. Were the

Elon Musk participates in the opening bell ceremony at the NASDAQ Marketsite with two of his children and his then fiancée Talulah Riley (second from right), in New York on 29 June 2010, on the day of Tesla's IPO.

Model S a conventional petrol-powered vehicle, it would be doing more than 160 km (100 miles) per gallon. The battery, the heaviest component of the car, is located between the axles, which gives the vehicle exceptional stability on the road. All the models are fast, the P100D being exceptionally so – it has an astonishing 0–60 mph time of 2.28 seconds, which for a while made it the fastest production vehicle in the world. Almost everything is digitally controlled by the central touchscreen, which has 24-hour internet connectivity. The connectivity brought a real customer value – if there was something wrong with the car's performance or functionality, customers would report it to Tesla and then Tesla engineers could log into the vehicle remotely and make the fix directly in the car's software, sometimes while the customer slept.

The system could also automatically navigate the driver to any Tesla charging station.

The innovations in the Model S kept on coming and suddenly the big carmakers seemed like lumbering dinosaurs, stumbling behind Tesla and trying to catch up. Musk's company also began building charging stations around the USA, these offering free charging to Tesla customers. For a time, Tesla would also offer a 90-second battery-swapping service at the charging stations, although that idea was eventually dropped, and 480-volt Tesla Supercharger stations offer the fastest way to charge Tesla vehicles.

What was truly astonishing about the Model S was some of the press plaudits. A review of the early production car by *Consumer Reports* gave an astounding review: 'This car performs better than anything we've ever tested before. Let me repeat that: Not just the best *electric* car, but the best car. It does just about everything really, really well.' Similarly, in 2019 the magazine *Motor Press* declared that the 2013 Model S was not only the 'Car of the Year', but also the superior vehicle of *all* the Cars of the Year over the magazine's 70-year history.

WORLD BEATER

With the Model S, Tesla's commercial trajectory banked sharply upward. But it went into an even steeper climb with the addition of subsequent models. The original logic of Tesla – that the sales of high-end vehicles would ultimately fund the development and production of more mass-market EVs – held good. In September 2015, the company launched the Model X, a mid-sized luxury sedan partly based on the Model S, but with the standout feature of 'falcon-wing doors' – a term coined by Musk. The doors, on

Elon Musk checks his phone in the Tesla store at Westfield Stratford City retail complex in London, UK, on 24 October 2013, with a Tesla Model S automobile next to him on display. Tesla not only revolutionized the design of electric vehicles, but also the way in which vehicles were sold to the public.

opening, rise up and then flatten out, and were designed (on Musk's visions) primarily to provide easy access for parents trying to get kids or shopping in the back seats, even with cars parked tightly on either side or with low garage ceilings.

But the real game-changer was the Model 3 compact sedan, which went to market in July 2017. Here was a true mass-market car – relatively affordable on middle-class budgets but offering all the unique qualities of a Tesla EV. Early press reviews were enthusiastic, seeing it as a new option to those otherwise tempted by a mid-range BMW, Audi or Mercedes. The car was unveiled on the morning of 31 March 2016, and within two days, Tesla had 232,000 reservations; within a week, that figure had risen to 325,000.

Once production issues were overcome, the Model 3 went on to become the world's best-selling EV. In August 2021, some media sources calculated that more than 1 million Model 3s had been sold. Furthermore, by this time Tesla had another best-selling model available, the Model Y, a compact crossover unveiled in 2019, with deliveries beginning in 2020, offering a less-expensive option than the Model X. (Observant readers might have noticed that the models 'S', 'X' and 'Y' nearly spell the word 'SEXY'. This, apparently, was intentional on Musk's part; the 'E' was taken when Ford blocked Tesla's use of 'Model E', saying it was too similar-sounding to Ford's original Model T. Tesla's Model 3, therefore, is essentially a Model E with the 'E' reversed to a '3'.) Model Y sales climbed past the 500,000 mark by the end of 2021. But before we think that Musk was slipping into becoming a conventional car CEO, we will now take a moment to explore another way in which Musk has challenged the outlook of an entire industry forever.

MUSK AS MARKETER

In May 2019, the digital marketing consultancy BrandTotal produced a report analysing the social media spend of some of the world's biggest car companies – Toyota, BMW, Honda, Audi, Ford, Infiniti, Cadillac, Porsche and Tesla – over a 30-day period. One of the stand-out conclusions of the report was that while almost all the car companies were spending heavily on paid advertising across the four major social media platforms (FacebBook, YouTube, Instagram and Twitter), Tesla was paying precisely zero dollars. And yet despite its complete lack of monetary ad investment, Tesla still had 2 million organic engagements on social media, only behind Porsche, which had 2.2 million, although they were a mix of both paid and organic. If we take the analysis back to 2015, other patterns emerge. According to a report by Global Equities Research for that year, Tesla's ad spend per vehicle sold was just $6 – not yet $0, but still laughably meagre. Note how this compared to some other major manufacturers:

Toyota – $248
Honda – $258
Porsche (VW) – $267
Cadillac (General Motors) – $1,163
Lexus (Toyota) – $1,168
Fiat (Fiat Chrysler) – $2,158
Lincoln (Ford) – $2,550
Jaguar – $3,325
(Hanley 2016)

Obviously, there are major differences in the sizes and competitiveness of the markets the individual carmakers contest, but the gulf between the Tesla costs and those of other makers cannot purely be reduced to these terms.

As in almost all his other business models, Elon Musk is a disruptor in advertising, largely because he has found powerful ways to avoid paying for publicity. This is astonishing when framed with industry comparisons. In 2019, the year of the BrandTotal report, Ford spent $3.6 billion, Toyota $1.5 billion and the relatively restrained BMW $300 million on advertising. It is worth asking, therefore, how Musk is transforming the model.

Historically, Musk's capabilities as a marketer have divided opinion. In the Zip2 and PayPal years, Musk's marketing was seen by many – inside and outside his companies – as rather hot-headed, making dramatic promises of launch dates and service breakthroughs that often stretched beyond the realities of delivery. (This has remained a criticism of Musk to this day.) But what was certain was that Musk could create a buzz about his businesses in a way that few others could. Musk is a prime exponent of what we today call 'CEO-led marketing', the personality, insights and promises of the leader being used to drive product information, create customers and generate 'buzz' and viral energy within the digital media domain.

Musk's undoubted dynamism, adventurism and innovation, in addition to his involved personal life and celebrity status, have generated a mass following of adoring fans, known as 'Muskateers', a dynamic and enthusiastic community through which Musk can deliver his marketing interactions. Note that Musk has more than 81 million followers on Twitter, only marginally fewer than Lady Gaga, Ariana Grande and Taylor Swift. Musk is an active and frequent tweeter. He genuinely engages with his followers, answering questions, leaving teasing hints of what is to come, connecting with people across all walks of life, but especially those with the same appetites for technology, innovation and entrepreneurship. An article in Businessinsider.com by Mark Matousek, published shortly after the Roadster sailed past Earth for the cameras, recognized Musk's accessible voice on social media:

> Musk has also shown a gift for building excitement through social media. He is one of the few CEOs with a Twitter account that doesn't feel as if it's written by a public-relations team, and his

candor is both endearing and effective. He responds to questions and concerns from Tesla customers, teases upcoming features, and cracks jokes, generating a significant amount of news coverage for his companies.

Furthermore, the content Musk talks about on Twitter is exciting, varied and charismatic, one minute chatting about his general thoughts on success or literature, the next probing obscure corners of aerospace engineering or physics. It is a lively and dynamic sphere, one equally electrified by Musk's celebrity – people are interested not only in what he does, but also in what he thinks, how he behaves, what he buys, what he reads.

Elon Musk ✓

@elonmusk

🗓 Joined June 2009

113 Following   **81.3M**

Twitter has been one of Musk's most powerful tools for disseminating his views, messages and product marketing, and his account is followed by more than 80 million people globally. In April 2022, he bought the Twitter company for $44 billion (at the time of writing, the purchase is pending approval by regulators).

Then there are Musk's big, demonstrative acts of marketing, the ones that set social media alight. At the summit of these is, surely, the launch of the Tesla Roadster into space in 2019, mentioned in the previous chapter. We should not see this moment purely as an expression of audacity, gaining publicity through shock and absurdity. Mark Wnek in *Advertising Age* declared that Musk was 'miles ahead of the rest' in reaching a younger demographic, acknowledging that where 'mere mortals scrabble about spending millions to fight each other over seconds of air time' Musk 'just executes his vision'.

But the Roadster launch also accrued many column inches in specialist space, technology and automotive magazines, heightening awareness of topics such as space exploration, the future of electric vehicles, the potential of autonomous technologies, all while attaching the Musk brand to the ideas. As so often with Musk's marketing, the media follows the conversation he creates and effectively does the marketing for him.

However, we should be careful about attempting, as many have done, to distil the 'Musk method of advertising and marketing', although there are certainly valuable lessons to be learned. I think the error is one of focus. While Musk certainly understands the power of social media and viral publicity, he also appreciates that ultimately it is customer satisfaction with the product that drives the success story. If the product is inferior, it ultimately won't gain commercial traction, no matter how much 'buzz' you might attempt to generate around it. The $0 ad spend at Tesla is not because money doesn't need to be spent on marketing, but the best marketing investment is to create a product people love, as Musk outlined in a TV interview:

What we really focus on in Tesla is – we put all the money into and attention into trying to make the product as compelling as possible, because I think that really the way to sell any product is through word of mouth. So if somebody gets the car, they really like it. Actually, the key is to have a product that people love and generally people, if they're at a party or talking to friends or whatever, you'll talk about the things that you love, but if you just like something, it's OK, you're not going to care that much. But if you really love it, you're going to talk, and then that will drive word of mouth. And that's basically how our sales have grown. We don't spend any money on advertising or endorsements, so if anyone buys our car they just bought it because they like the car.

We could perhaps make a parallel between Musk's focus on product development and Jeff Bezos's extreme customer focus. Both essentially come from the same angle of attack – make the customer happy first and foremost, whether with a product or a service, and to a large degree the rest will take care of itself.

MUSK, THE TWITTERVERSE AND POLITICS

For Musk, Twitter has been one of the key tools in his extraordinary marketing power, giving his voice a deep and broad reach into an ever-growing army of loyal followers, while enticing business leaders, analysts and the media with cryptic hints of future plans. But the mass influence he wields through Twitter has been questioned and challenged from several quarters, not least the US government itself. On 7 August 2018, Musk tweeted the following message: 'Am considering taking Tesla private at $420. Funding secured.' Given that Musk had taken Tesla public just eight years previously, this was clearly major news, albeit broken through a rather informal channel for its import. The same day, Musk sent a lengthier email to his employees spelling out his financial vision for the company. As always, such documents open additional windows of understanding on to how Musk operates as a businessman. He explained to his employees that 'a final decision has not yet been made, but the reason for doing this is all about creating the environment for Tesla to operate best'. He first set the context, outlining his view that Tesla was a company with its strategic eye on distant horizons, and the 'wild swings in our stock price that can be a major distraction for everyone working at Tesla, all of whom are shareholders'. Musk further explained that being a public company makes Tesla more beholden to performance within a quarterly earnings cycle, rather than to more considered future goals. 'I fundamentally believe that we are at our best when everyone is focused on executing, when we can remain focused on our long-term mission, and when there are not perverse incentives for people to try to harm what we're all trying to achieve.' He also pointed to SpaceX as the 'perfect example' of the efficiencies that can be attained by a privately owned company.

In the second, lengthier part of his email, Musk laid out in detail what this all meant for Tesla employees. He had no intention of merging Tesla and SpaceX. He also iterated that the possibility of taking Tesla private 'has nothing to do with accumulating control for myself' – he stated that taking the company private would have little effect on his current 20 per cent ownership of the company. He signed off: 'A private Tesla would ultimately be an enormous opportunity for all of us. Either way, the future is very bright and we'll keep fighting to achieve our mission.' According to the email, only a shareholder vote stood between opportunity and reality.

Within this email, therefore, Musk's habitual perspectives are reinforced – keeping focus on the long-term vision; putting product development above short-term financial considerations; not allowing external pressures to distort long-term development. It was persuasive stuff. One organization that was definitely not impressed with Musk's tweet, however, was the US Securities and Exchange Commission (SEC). This venerable instrument of the US government exercised a three-part regulatory mission (in its own words) to 'protect investors; maintain fair, orderly, and efficient markets; facilitate capital formation'. As markets reacted to the Musk tweet, the SEC fired up a complaint and investigation against Musk, on the following grounds:

> The SEC's complaint alleged that, in truth, Musk knew that the potential transaction was uncertain and subject to numerous contingencies. Musk had not discussed specific deal terms, including price, with any potential financing partners, and his statements about the possible transaction lacked an adequate basis in fact. According to the SEC's complaint, Musk's misleading tweets caused Tesla's stock price to jump by over six percent on August 7, and led to significant market disruption.

The SEC was tacitly recognizing the market influence that even a single tweet from Musk can exert. The following September, Musk and the SEC came to a settlement, with neither Musk nor Tesla either admitting or denying the charges. But the terms of the settlement were severe:

1. Musk will step down as Tesla's Chairman and be replaced by an independent Chairman. Musk will be ineligible to be re-elected Chairman for three years;
2. Tesla will appoint a total of two new independent directors to its board;
3. Tesla will establish a new committee of independent directors and put in place additional controls and procedures to oversee Musk's communications;
4. Musk and Tesla will each pay a separate $20 million penalty. The $40 million in penalties will be distributed to harmed investors under a court-approved process.

As part of the third bullet point (according to press reports), lawyers would scrutinize Musk's tweets before they were posted, in order to ensure that they conformed with the settlement requirements. But as time would show, this was by no means the end of the struggle between the SEC and Musk.

Musk has described himself as a 'free speech absolutist'. Notably, this phrase was used in a tweet posted on 5 March 2022, during the opening weeks of the Russian invasion of Ukraine, in which Musk argued: 'Starlink has been told by some governments (not Ukraine) to block Russian news sources. We will not do so unless at gunpoint. Sorry to be a free speech absolutist.' For Musk, the preservation of people's ability to say what they think is sacrosanct, thus following the settlement with the SEC in 2018, many were interested to see how the conditions would affect his Twitter activity. From the user's point of view, not too significantly. Musk has continued to muse and reflect freely, and this brought continuing friction with the SEC. In February 2019, the SEC accused Musk of contempt of court by tweeting about expected Tesla production figures without first seeking the approval of company lawyers, a charge that Musk countered angrily. Relations between Musk and the SEC went even lower, Musk referring to the SEC as the 'Shortseller Enrichment Commission' in another tweet (4 October 2018). Then, in November 2021, the SEC issued a subpoena to Tesla seeking information about 'governance processes around compliance with the SEC settlement, as amended'.

On 17 February 2022, Musk and Tesla pushed back more forcibly – Musk's lawyers issued a legal complaint against the SEC, stating that the government agency had 'gone beyond the pale', accusing the body of failing to pay Tesla shareholders the $40 million it had collected from the 2018 settlement and arguing that the SEC 'has been devoting its formidable resources to endless, unfounded investigations into Mr. Musk and Tesla'. In a subsequent letter, the SEC defended itself against the accusations, saying that it was behaving consistently in line with the expectations of the 2018 agreement.

As I am writing this book, the tension between the SEC and Elon Musk shows little sign of abating. On 11 February, a contributor to Musk's Twitter (Earl of Frunk Puppy) posted a comment: 'Tesla drawing attention from the CDFEH [California Department of Fair Employment and Housing], NHTSA [National Highway Traffic Safety Administration], SEC, and CA DMV [California Department of Motor Vehicles] all at the same time because they are upsetting unions, legacy auto, the oil industry, and autonomous driving companies and not paying for ads or buying politicians.' To which Musk replied succinctly: 'Exactly'.

This situation perhaps reflects an almost inevitable conflict between powerful private individuals and the government, a relationship that oscillates erratically according to the political colours of the administration in power and the public leverage of the business leader. Musk is undoubtedly one of the planet's most influential private citizens and is likely to remain so for the foreseeable future. His core interests overlap squarely with many of those of the US government and international polities – space, transport, finance, energy, culture – and thus he will be forever under the government spotlight.

Although Musk is a driven entrepreneur, and like most entrepreneurs doesn't appreciate political roadblocks dropped across the path of progress, it would be lazy to characterize him as a simple free-wheeling capitalist. Musk's political views, if they can be discerned, appear nuanced and pragmatic, rather than visibly aligned in one particular direction. From the public statements he has given, he appears largely centrist in outlook, describing himself as 'half Democrat, half Republican', and pro-democracy but with 'socialist' sympathies. But he certainly understands the importance of access to political movers and shakers. In 2012, the Sunlight Foundation, the non-profit research organization advocating open government, published a report exploring Musk's political contributions. It claimed that since its foundation in 2002, SpaceX had spent 'more than $4 million lobbying Congress and given more than $800,000 in political contributions'. In November 2021, CNBC reported that SpaceX and Tesla had spent more than $2 million on lobbying since the beginning of 2021. The author is unable to verify these claims, but perhaps attempting to do so is not the smoking gun it might seem to be. Given the nature of Musk's projects and businesses, some degree of political buy-in is essential to the realization of his work. This is not an argument in favour of untrammelled and egregious political lobbying, but rather an acceptance that given Musk's domains it would be hard to see how seeking government understanding and support could *not* be involved at some level.

The levels of political access are highly variable, however. At the time of writing, for example, relations between Musk and President Joe Biden seem to have hit rock bottom. Musk has made repeated complaints that President Biden has largely avoided referring to Tesla in any discussions of the electric car market, despite Tesla being the largest manufacturer of EVs in the USA, by a huge margin. (By 2020, about 80 per cent of EVs manufactured in the USA came from Tesla factories.) In August 2021, President Biden invited executives from General Motors, Ford and Chrysler (collectively known as the 'Big Three' carmakers) to a signing ceremony of an executive order urging that US auto manufacturers produce more EVs. Musk and Tesla were not invited, a decision about which Musk commented: 'Yeah, seems odd that Tesla wasn't invited.' (Musk subsequently argued that this situation was especially curious given that GM sold just 26 electric vehicles in the fourth quarter of 2021, a quarter in which Tesla sold 308,600 of an annual total of 936,172.) The political logjam seemed to be broken on 6 April, when Biden administration officials met with Musk and other automotive leaders to discuss electric vehicles and charging infrastructure.

All this being said, when it comes to matters of the economy specifically, Musk appears to like the government to stay in its proper lane. In the following quotation, given during a TV interview, Musk provided a neat definition of what that lane should be, and where government could be served:

> I'm generally a fan of like minimal government interference in the economy. Like the government should be kind of like the referee but not the player and there should not be too many referees. But there is an exception, which is when there's an unpriced externality such as the CO_2 capacity of the oceans and atmosphere. So when you have an unpriced externality then the normal market mechanisms do not work and then the government's job is to intervene. And the best way to intervene is to assign a proper price to whatever the common good is that's being consumed, and there should be a tax on carbon, you know, if the bad thing is carbon.

Musk recognizes here that some crucial issues facing humanity sit outside the purview of market forces, and of necessity need to be handled by national governments. But overall, Musk sees it as important for the government to rule its people with a light touch, staying out of the daily operations of lives and business. He put it succinctly in a tweet on 2 December 2021: 'In general, I believe government should rarely impose its will upon the people, and, when doing so, should aspire to maximize their cumulative happiness. That said, I would prefer to stay out of politics.'

Musk might prefer to stay out of politics, but we have already seen how difficult that is, not least because even the briefest of his tweets can spark the most intense speculation and media interest. Musk certainly understands the waves his Twitter account can set in motion. On 14 March 2022, in an announcement that sent an earthquake through the media landscape, it was revealed that Musk had purchased nearly $3 billion worth of Twitter stock, making him the largest shareholder in the company with a 9.2 per cent share. The day after the revelation, Twitter's CEO, Parag Agrawal, then disclosed that Musk had been invited on to the company's board of directors, an offer that apparently Musk accepted. Then came an abrupt about-turn. On 11 April, Agrawal explained in a tweet that 'Elon has decided not to join our board.' The tweet also posted the letter sent to unsettled Twitter employees, and while it gave no detail about the decision it did state that 'Elon is our biggest shareholder and we will remain open to his input.' After news of the U-turn broke, Musk put out a cryptic tweet consisting of nothing but a hand-over-mouth emoji.

The media went into overdrive in its interpretation of events. One crucial factor in the mix, and possibly the driving force behind Musk's investment, was that Musk had publicly hinted at a dissatisfaction with Twitter's direction. In a tweet of 5 April, Musk stated how he was 'Looking forward to working with Parag & Twitter to make significant improvements to Twitter in coming months!' Some of the potential 'improvements', according to media trawling of Musk's earlier Twitter comments (some of which were subsequently deleted), appeared to include: making Twitter ad-free; converting the San Francisco headquarters into a homeless shelter; cutting the price of the Twitter Blue premium subscription service, plus giving the option to pay via the cryptocurrency Dogecoin. Also significant was a posting on 25 March, in which Musk presented a poll question: 'Free speech is essential to a functioning democracy. Do you believe Twitter rigorously adheres to this principle?' Of the 2,035,924 votes that came back, 70.4 per cent voted 'No'. The next day, a follower asked Musk if he would consider developing a new social media platform himself, to which he replied: 'Am giving serious thought to this'. Later (4 April), he issued another poll: 'Do you want an edit button?', referring to the ability to return to a tweet and edit it after it had been posted; 73.6 per cent of more than 4.4 million voters replied 'Yes'.

It feels clear that Musk wants to have a shaping influence over Twitter. Ironically, as the press quickly pointed out, not going on to the board of directors could actually give him better tools to wield this influence, as by rejecting the board seat Musk would no longer be limited to a maximum 14.9 per cent stake – he could potentially become the majority shareholder. Just days after I wrote the last sentence, Musk made a $43 billion offer to buy Twitter outright, saying that 'I think it's very important for there to be an inclusive area for free speech'. Twitter subsequently accepted the acquisition, raised slightly to $44 billion.

The situation is still very much playing out as this book goes to press, with Musk apparently withdrawing his bid for Twitter, although it remains to be seen whether this is the end of the story or is simply part of an evolving strategy. Time will therefore tell whether Musk eventually adds Twitter to his portfolio, but however it pans out, social media will certainly be a critical strand within Musk's commercial future. What is apparent is that in Twitter especially, Musk has found and mastered a uniquely pervasive platform for his views and announcements, and for his exceptionally effective strategies of indirect marketing.

EV FUTURES

A year after the Model S went on sale, Tesla finally made its first profit, with a quarterly revenue of $562 million (Vance 2015: 271).

But how times change. In 2021, Tesla's total revenue was $53.82 billion, which in itself was a 71 per cent increase over the previous year. In October 2021, Tesla's market capitalization was valued at a stratospheric $1 trillion. The company now has six major factories around the world (in 2020 alone Tesla manufactured 500,000 vehicles). Instead of customers going to classic car showrooms to view Teslas, they can simply buy them online and have them delivered to their door or collected from a delivery centre. Tesla has an estimated 80 per cent vertical integration, a degree of control over the production process virtually unheard of in automotive engineering. Early predictions that Musk was going to be destroyed by the big carmakers have been quashed comprehensively. What's more, new vehicles are on their way, such as the strikingly angular and futuristic Cybertruck, pitched by Tesla as having 'better utility than a truck with more performance than a sports car', and the Tesla Semi, a full-scale lorry powered by four independent motors.

One of Tesla's most revolutionary R&D engagements is its pursuit of 'self-driving' technologies. In September 2014, it introduced the 'Autopilot' system capability on all its cars. This advanced assisted driving feature, delivered through powerful onboard software allied to multiple cameras and sensors around the vehicle, could take over certain driving functions from the human operator, such as: parking; steering and cruising within a driving lane, automatically accelerating or braking; and making optimal navigation decisions (such as steering towards recommended highway interchanges). Autopilot features, according to the company's website, still 'require active driver supervision and do not make the vehicle autonomous'. Yet Tesla is, at the time of writing, on the brink of

Elon Musk treats robotics with both optimism and caution, the latter particularly in relation to artificial intelligence. Here he examines a robot arm during a tour of the new Tesla Motors auto plant in Fremont, California, in 2010.

delivering full self-driving (FSD) capability. The Tesla site clarifies that 'All new Tesla cars have the hardware needed in the future for full self-driving in almost all circumstances. The system is designed to be able to conduct short and long distance trips with no action required by the person in the driver's seat.'

Tesla is not alone in pursuing autonomous driving technologies, nor is Musk naive about the challenge of achieving safe, competent FSD – the deaths of a small number of car drivers incurred while using Autopilot mode have raised some questions about the relationship between driver responsibility and autonomous technologies. In Musk's interview with Lex Fridman, when asked about the problem of self-driving, he reflected after a pause:

I thought that the self-driving problem would be hard, but it is harder than I thought. [. . .] It's a lot of friggin' software man. A lot of smart lines of code. For sure, in order to create an accurate vector space [. . .] you are coming from image space which is this flow of photons going to the cameras. So you have this massive bit stream in image space. And you have to effectively compress a mass of bit stream corresponding to photos that knocked off an electron in a camera sensor and turn that bit stream into vector space. By vector space I mean like you've got cars and humans and lane lines and curves and traffic lights and that kind of thing. Once you have an accurate vector space the control problem is similar to that of a video game, like *Grand Theft Auto* or *Cyberpunk*, if you have accurate vector space. [. . .] Having accurate vector space is very difficult.

Many hurdles are to be crossed before we are being whisked between destinations in a car that drives itself, our lives and safety transferred into the digital hands of software and sensors. But given Musk's now undoubted ability to transform a technological future, it is surely just a matter of time.

The Tesla journey has not been plain sailing. As with all Musk's ventures, he has garnered controversy along the way. Tesla as a company faced accusations of sexual harassment from a small group of female employees in 2021, an accusation in which they implicated Musk's own behaviours and outlooks. There have been labour disputes over health and safety violations and concerns about financial reporting and anti-competitive practices. There have been accusations of racial discrimination at some of Tesla's plants. Musk's defiant views on Covid-19 stay-at-home orders also brought clashes with authorities and media. But however the world relates to Musk and Tesla, and however justified some accusations, both the company and its CEO keeps their eyes on the horizon, showing no signs of slowing down. In terms of the future, Musk's foot is not coming off the (electric) accelerator pedal.

CHAPTER 5
THE FULL PICTURE

The accumulation of wealth and power has been likened to the flow of a river. The river by itself offers utility as it journeys to the sea – providing drinking and washing water to the communities that border the river, powering hydroelectric facilities, offering a transit route for boat traffic. But as the volume and flow rate of a river increases, more opportunities arise to tap off that water into separate distributaries. These minor streams or rivers then gain their own functions over a greater area – crop irrigation is a good example. Thus, the distributaries begin with, and to a degree depend upon, the main river, but over time they acquire an independent value all of their own.

Applied to commercial expansion and the growth of wealth, the analogy is transparent – the more money is flowing through the river, the more opportunities there are to tap off some of that wealth into new own wealth-generating streams. It is essentially a visualization of the old adage, 'Money begets money'.

Taking Elon Musk as a case study, we can clearly see how his commercial expansion deepened, quickened and branched out over time. The capital generated from Zip2 beget X.com and then PayPal; PayPal's eventual buy-out provided the means to develop SpaceX and Tesla; both of these companies have their own sub-strands, with SpaceX diversified from communication satellites to Mars missions, and Tesla from EVs to, as we shall see, solar panels and energy storage. In this chapter, we shall widen our focus to take in some of the other corners of Musk's entrepreneurial outreach, new flows of water that in themselves might turn into the rivers of the future.

What is distinctive about Musk's commercial and intellectual empire, however, is the fundamental integration of all its elements into what truly matters to Musk. Musk is not a scattergun venture capitalist, with a 'diverse portfolio' of unrelated but profitable businesses. Instead, his enterprises form a fairly coherent jigsaw when looked at from a distance. Energy, space, transport and computer-aided intelligence might seem like siloed ventures, but for Musk they share the same mental space, while also opening up constant possibilities for interaction. Fundamentally, Musk's portfolio is about optimizing the human future through technology.

SOLARCITY AND TESLA ENERGY

Elon Musk is a big believer in clean energy. We have seen this in Tesla's pursuit of the optimal EV, and the constant investment in energy storage research, with ever more efficient generations of batteries. But to charge a battery, you need a power input in the first place, and in the modern age that energy often comes from a power station burning fossil fuels. This does not mean that there is no net saving of energy in EVs; power stations can produce energy with far greater efficiency than the sum of individual vehicles. But the next stage in the evolution of clean energy is to wean ourselves off fossil-fuel power generation altogether. One avenue that Musk advocates is nuclear energy, the risks of which are greatly outweighed by the advantages it offers for clean and sustainable energy. Responding to fears of a Europe-wide gas shortage following the Russian invasion of Ukraine in February 2022, Musk tweeted on 6 March: 'Hopefully it is now extremely obvious that Europe should restart dormant nuclear power stations and increase power output of existing ones. This is critical to national and international security.' But another major strand of Musk's environmental thinking is solar power, which in his view greatly exceeds even the possibilities of nuclear:

> It's worth noting, I'm not sure if people are aware of this, but the world could be powered many times over by solar if you had enough battery capacity to pair with it. Many times . . . like a thousand, it's literally true. The amount of energy that reaches the Earth from the Sun is staggeringly high. We have this enormous fusion generator in the sky that is lobbing out vast amounts of energy. And I'm talking about just using land area, I mean it's really amazing. In fact, here's a little tip. If you take a nuclear plant and you take its current output and compared that to just taking solar panels and putting solar panels on the area used by the nuclear power plant – because these typically have a big keep-out zone, maybe five kilometres or thereabouts, where building houses of any kind of dense office or a housing space, usually people don't want to do that. So there's quite a big keep-out zone, and when you factor the keep-out zone into account, the solar panels put on that area will typically generate more power than the nuclear power plant.

Musk's long-standing belief in solar energy has morphed into another of his major enterprises, which began its life back in a company called SolarCity.

Much like Tesla, SolarCity first inches into existence in the hands of others, but with critical financial and intellectual involvement from Musk. In 2004, Musk made a suggestion to two of his cousins – the brothers Lyndon and Peter – that solar power presented a potentially lucrative and ethically worthwhile future opportunity. The Rive brothers had already run a successful data management company called Everdream and were receptive to a fresh ambition. Thus, on 4 July 2006, after a period of reflection and research, Peter and Lyndon Rive founded SolarCity, with Musk as the company chairman and the biggest single investor, with about 30 per cent equity in the business.

The commercial model of SolarCity ran as follows. The brothers would buy in solar panels (hence there were no manufacturing costs), install them and provide the software (developed by themselves) for running the system. Here was the crucial part – the customer would pay no up-front costs for buying the panels, which in 2008 could be about $20,000 for an average house. Instead, they would lease the panels for a period of years, paying a fixed monthly rate. Financing was provided by Morgan Stanley, via SolarCity.

Solar leasing become the dominant model for the US domestic solar power industry in the USA, and SolarCity was, initially, a resounding success. By 2013, it had become the leading solar residential installer in the USA and was also a major commercial supplier, providing solar installations for, among others, Walmart, Intel and the US military. The company had the scale to purchase several other big-time solar power companies and, by 2015, employed more than 15,000 people. By 2016, SolarCity had provided solar installations for more than 325,000 customers.

Musk had been interacting with SolarCity from the outset and connecting it with his other lines of business. In a Tesla blog on 2 August 2006, Musk posted an intriguing document entitled 'The Secret Tesla Motors Master Plan (just between you and me)'. In it, he laid down at some length the energy arguments for his EVs, but near the end there was a further section sub-headed 'Becoming Energy Positive'. The first paragraph linked out to SolarCity:

> I should mention that Tesla Motors will be co-marketing sustainable energy products from other companies along with the car. For example, among other choices, we will be offering a modestly sized and priced solar panel from SolarCity, a photovoltaics company (where I am also the principal financier). This system can be installed on your roof in an out of the way location, because of its small size, or set up as a carport and will generate about 50 miles per day of electricity.

Solar panel installation would be just the beginning of the Tesla/SolarCity synergy. In 2011, for a time it looked likely that SolarCity would be building electric charging stations for Tesla EVs in California, although this idea was replaced by Tesla's own-brand charging stations the following year. In 2014, however, SolarCity began to sell powerful battery storage packs, manufactured by Tesla, to business and domestic customers. Tesla had itself, since 2012, been selling industrial battery storage units to industry, a growing commercial arena to be supported by the building of a new lithium ion battery factory in Nevada, called Giga Nevada (this would open in 2016). In April 2013, Musk announced a new Tesla subsidiary, Tesla Energy, which would focus on the battery supply market, developing two major products – the Powerpack for industrial use and the new Powerwall for domestic use. (Tesla Energy also launched the Tesla Megapack in 2019, a unit capable of storing 3 megawatts of electricity.)

Batteries, it should be mentioned, are a critical strand of Musk's environmental thinking, as banal as they might seem to us. Think well beyond the clip-in batteries we slot into our household devices. In September 2020, Musk spoke of humanity's need to push battery storage technology and solutions at a rate never before seen, giving homes and businesses the means to store energy derived from renewable sources like solar and wind, and use it during those moments when the supply drops, or sell it back to the grid.

The rolling good times for SolarCity were interrupted brutally in 2015–16. Wider legislative and market changes in the US solar industry hit profits. The company suffered reductions in new customers and reduced income streams, compelling it to make more than 3,000 employees (20 per cent of the company) redundant in 2016. But then, on 1 August 2016, Tesla made the announcement that it was buying SolarCity for $2.6 billion. SolarCity would now be absorbed into Tesla Energy, thus coming directly under the control of Tesla CEO, Elon Musk. Lyndon and Peter Rive both left the company in 2017.

Musk's acquisition of SolarCity made sense on several levels. Not only was it a company in which Musk had a founding role, and that had commercial connections with Tesla, but it also offered a logical expansion of Musk's clean-energy vision, with the addition of solar power. Musk and his companies had also injected a great deal of money into SolarCity; in 2015, SpaceX purchased $165 million in bonds from the company, the only time to that date that

SpaceX had ever invested in a publicly traded company (Higgins 2021: 215). In a blog post dated 20 July 2016, Musk explained the merger:

> We can't do this well if Tesla and SolarCity are different companies, which is why we need to combine and break down the barriers inherent to being separate companies. That they are separate at all, despite similar origins and pursuit of the same overarching goal of sustainable energy, is largely an accident of history. Now that Tesla is ready to scale Powerwall and SolarCity is ready to provide highly differentiated solar, the time has come to bring them together.

But the purchase of SolarCity has been one of the more controversial business decisions of Musk's career. Tesla's stock valuation almost immediately dropped $3.38 billion, as investors were spooked by the acquisition of a company and an industry that were on the financial ropes. A group of major Tesla shareholders began legal proceedings against Musk and Tesla Inc., claiming that SolarCity had major liquidity issues – essentially it was going broke – and that Musk knew that but did not share the information during the acquisition approval process. Musk was accused of securing the deal more for his own benefit than that of Tesla and its shareholders. The case is still in process in April 2022, at the time of writing this book. Musk has personally been in the spotlight and has vigorously defended the deal. On 18 January 2022, Reuters reported that during closing arguments the aggrieved shareholders 'urged a judge on Tuesday to find Elon Musk coerced the company's board into a 2016 deal for SolarCity and asked that the chief executive be ordered to pay the electric vehicle company one of the largest judgments ever of $13 billion' (Hals 2022). The case awaits its resolution.

The move into solar power has brought other challenges for Elon Musk. These include Tesla being sued by Walmart in 2019 for fires caused by faulty solar panels fitted to the roofs of seven of its stores. (Walmart dropped the case in late 2019 after agreeing a settlement.) The energy business was also tough. Reuters reported in November 2019 that 'Tesla's solar panel market share has been falling, prompting the Palo Alto, California-based company to cut its sales force. Revenue from Tesla's energy generation and storage operations from January to September fell 7% from a year earlier to $1.1 billion' (Stempel 2019).

Elon Musk emerges from court for the SolarCity trial in Wilmington, Delaware, on 12 July 2021, having been questioned about Tesla Inc.'s more than $2 billion acquisition of SolarCity in 2016. Musk's rise to success has not been without regular legal challenges.

There were also significant problems regarding Tesla Energy's development of a solar shingle (photovoltaic panels designed to look like and function as conventional roofing materials). Although the 'Solar Roof' was demonstrated in 2016 (on the set of *Desperate Housewives*, as it happened), it was subsequently revealed that the product was not working properly. By 2020, the product was still struggling to achieve production volumes. A Bloomberg article on 23 June 2021 carried the headline: 'Tesla's Solar Rollout is a Bust – And a Fixation for Elon' (Hull 2021).

Tesla Energy might appear to be one of Musk's more struggling ventures. Yet if history has proved one thing about Musk, it is that he has the tenacity to defy even the harshest of critics and eventually produce breakthrough results that confound almost everyone. Growth is once again appearing – in 2020, the company installed 205 megawatts (MW) of solar systems and 3,022 MW of electrical storage, but in 2021 those figures jumped significantly to 345 MW and 3,992 MW respectively. Time will tell whether Tesla Energy's most influential days are yet to come.

GOING UNDERGROUND

On 17 December 2016, Elon Musk posted the following on Twitter: 'Traffic is driving me nuts. Am going to build a tunnel boring machine and just start digging...' From anyone else, this would have been nothing but weary humour, but for a man with the vision and means of Musk, it signalled the beginning of a bold new venture. This time, instead of gazing into space or riding on the roads, Musk was looking to go underground, seeing another future of transportation beneath the Earth's surface. On 17 December 2017, he announced that he was forming The Boring Company (TBC).

The humour in the name, the inspiration of Musk's then-wife Talulah Riley, hinted at the initially casual (relatively speaking) nature of the project at first. But even though Musk would describe TBC as more of a 'personal hobby', accounting for 2–3 per cent of his time, he still formed a team who attacked the project with gusto. In fact, even before the formation of TBC, Musk had a go at underground tunnelling. The journalist Neil Strauss, writing for *Rolling Stone* magazine, stated that during one of his interview visits with Musk at SpaceX Hawthorne, CA, he noted that employees were rushing around to move their cars from a staff car park. The reason: Musk had asked them how long it would take for them to relocate their vehicles to another parking location for the foreseeable future. Their answer: two weeks. Musk's reply:

Elon Musk addresses journalists during an unveiling event for The Boring Company Hawthorne test tunnel in Hawthorne, California, on 18 December 2018. Musk explained that he was aiming to transfer both tunnel drilling and urban transport.

'Let's get started today and see what's the biggest hole we can dig between now and Sunday afternoon, running 24 hours a day.' Three hours later, the cars were gone, and Musk's engineering team started cracking the surface (Strauss 2017).

Soon, TBC was a major industrial venture in its own right, one that was plugged into the network of Musk's wider technological ambitions. Initially, the company was formed as part of SpaceX, but in 2018 it became a separate business, with Musk holding 90 per cent of the equity, the remainder in the hands of key employees. (Later, 6 per cent of the equity also went to SpaceX.) But what was the purpose of TBC? The overarching goals are captured by the company website, whose home page declares (as of 19 April 2022): 'The Boring Company creates safe, fast-to-dig, and low-cost transportation, utility, and freight tunnels. The mission: solve traffic, enable rapid point-to-point transportation and transform cities.' It was clear that Musk was thinking big again, but as always, there was a logic at play.

Musk has conceded that the development of EVs will do nothing to alleviate the global problem of urban traffic congestion; in fact, EVs could make it worse by ultimately developing a travel option that is cheaper than public transport. Elevated highways can only be built so high, and aerial vehicles are not realistic for mass transport. Tunnels, however, can be dug in great layers of highways through the deep substrata; Musk has pointed out that the deepest coal mines are more than a mile deep, thus tunnelling has a huge three-dimensional space to explore. If traffic is diverted into tunnels, then cities can become more beautiful, peaceful places. The tunnel traffic would, furthermore, be ordered but fast (Musk has mused on an upper figure of 241 km/h/150 mph), autonomous driving technologies replacing stop–start queues with smooth, orderly and congestion-free movement. Tunnel traffic would also be sheltered from external weather, there would be no noise pollution on the surface, and the multi-layer roads would not bisect neighbourhoods and green spaces. 'Traffic and congestion will become a thing of the past,' according to TBC.

What Musk was not proposing, however, was that he develop a tunnelling company just like any other. Instead, he is aiming to change the tunnelling industry and its associated engineering with all the revolutionary spirit he has applied to other ventures. The first tunnel built by TBC was a 1.8 km (1.14 mile)-long R&D Hawthorne Test Tunnel, which ran out from the SpaceX property. The narrow, clean and glowing tunnel space was unveiled to the press in December 2018. At the launch event, Musk explained more about this thinking on tunnels, including how to make their construction much cheaper and much faster. The present situation, he outlined with reference to a slide presentation, is that tunnelling is slow – about three to six months per mile, which he pointed out was 14 times slower than the movement of a snail – and hugely expensive, at up to \$1 billion per mile. TBC would do things differently. Major innovations would include:

1. Smaller-diameter tunnels – the tunnels will be built specifically for EVs, and the lack of exhaust gases and the absence of fume extraction systems mean that tunnels' diameters can be shrunk down, meaning less waste and quicker excavation.
2. Standardized diameters of tunnel-boring machines (TBMs), to aid logistical efficiency.

3. TBMs that combine tunnelling and reinforcement in a single process (most TBMs have to stop frequently to allow other crews to install the reinforcements).

4. A TBM with three times the cutting power of typical industry machines.

5. Re-use of the extracted dirt – the dirt can be converted into bricks and sold, with the potential for brick sales to cover the cost of the tunnelling.

6. Heavy automation of the tunnelling process to improve efficiency and logistics.

Elon Musk inspects a heat shield assembly at the SpaceX Hawthorne facility. His title of 'chief engineer' within SpaceX is no vanity title – Musk is a serious scientist and engineer and has been hands on with many aspects of the space programme development.

The innovations have borne fruit. The Hawthorne tunnel was completed for less than $10 million. Then in May 2019, TBC won a $48.7 million contract to build an underground loop system to take people around the expanded 200-acre Las Vegas Convention Center (LVCC). The LVCC Loop is a three-station, 2.7 km (1.7 mile)-long installation of twin tunnels that links the LVCC West Hall with the existing campus. TBC publicity explains that: 'LVCC Loop opened in April 2021 for the Mecum Motorcycle Auction and has operated at all subsequent conventions. At SEMA 2021, LVCC Loop transported between 24,000 and 26,000 passengers per day. At CES 2022, LVCC Loop transported between 14,000 and 17,000 passengers per day, with an average ride time of less than two minutes and average wait time of less than 15 seconds.' The passengers are taken along the route by Tesla Model 3 and Model Y vehicles. However, TBC's plans for Las Vegas are far greater. The Resorts World–LVCC Connector will link Resorts World on the Las Vegas Strip directly to the LVCC; Phase 1 building work has already been completed at the time of writing. Construction is also currently underway for the even more ambitious 'Vegas Loop', a 47 km (29 mile)-long tunnel network that 'will include LVCC Loop and any future service extensions including those to casinos along the Strip, Harry Reid International Airport, Allegiant Stadium, downtown Las Vegas, and eventually to Los Angeles. Vegas Loop will provide fast and convenient transportation to the Las Vegas community, its visitors, and beyond.'

Where TBC will go remains to be seen. Certainly, the technological boundaries of tunnelling are being tested by Musk's company. Its massive continuous-mining 'Prufrock' TBM (all the TBMs are named after poems or plays) is a supreme piece of TBC-developed equipment, able to start digging a 3.6 m (12 ft) tunnel within 48 hours of arrival on site, going straight down from the surface to remove the need to dig expensive launch pits in advance. TBC states that the 'medium-term goal' for Prufrock 'is to exceed 1/10 of human walking speed, which is 7 miles per day'.

The most ambitious TBC vision, though, is the Hyperloop, a regional/long-haul transport system in which passengers are whisked around the country in autonomous electric pods at speeds of more than 966 km/h (600 mph) by means of magnetic propulsion in a special sealed low-pressure tunnel that reduces wind resistance.

Musk is endlessly interested in innovation, especially when it emerges from young and dynamic talent. Here he studies the HyperXite team (University of California Irvine) pod during the SpaceX Hyperloop competition in Hawthorne, California in January 2017. Students from 30 colleges and universities across the United States and internationally took part in testing their pods on a 1.25 km-long Hyperloop track at the SpaceX headquarters.

Development of a SpaceX Hyperloop test track began in 2015 and the track reached its full length by 2016. Not everyone, including many engineering critics, is convinced by TBC's claims and ambitions. But Musk has never proved to be an individual daunted by professional scepticism.

DIGITAL HORIZONS

Given Elon Musk's deeply techie background and interests, it would be easy to assume that all high-end advances in computer technology meet his approval. Yet his viewpoints are more nuanced than that, not least with regard to artificial intelligence. Musk has publicly stated a belief in the power and advantages of AI, and an enthusiasm for its development, but is cautious when AI is married to robotics. With allusions to a *Terminator*-style robotic takeover, Musk has expressed fears that driving ahead blindly with AI-powered robotics would lead to machines with abilities far superior to our own and which may eventually dominate us entirely, or worse:

> If AI had a goal, and humanity just happens to be in the way, it will destroy humanity as a matter of course, without even thinking about it, no hard feelings. It's just like if we are building a road and an ant hill happens to be in the way. We don't hate ants, we're just building a road, and so – goodbye ant hill!

With more moderate language, he expressed similar sentiments in 2017 during a meeting of the National Governors Association, a Washington, DC-based nonpartisan political organization: 'Robots will be able to do everything better than us. I have exposure to the most cutting edge AI, and I think people should be really concerned by it.'

Musk's concerns about AI have led him practically in two main directions. First, in December 2015, Musk and a group of other investors set up OpenAI, a research organization that, in its own mission statement, 'conducts fundamental, long-term research toward the creation of safe AGI' [artificial general intelligence]. Together, the investors pledged $1 billion to the programme, and although Musk resigned from the board in 2018, he continues to make financial contributions.

OpenAI has a fascinating range of projects on its books, from advances in natural language AI (such as a computer creating an image purely from a textual description) to developing neural networks competent enough for a robotic hand to solve a Rubik's Cube. But returning to Musk's views on AI, what is perhaps most interesting is how Musk sees the future integration between humans and AI, at the level of biology itself. Given his concerns about where unrestricted AI might take us, surprisingly his answer is not to retreat from AI, but rather to bring humans closer to it, in a more symbiotic and therefore controlling position with technology. In December 2015, he told the *Seattle Times* that 'what is the best thing we can do to ensure the future is good? We could sit on the sidelines or we can encourage regulatory oversight, or we could participate with the right structure with people who care deeply about developing AI in a way that is safe and is beneficial to humanity.'

One of the main expressions of Musk's relationship to future-forward AI is Neuralink. Musk co-founded this neuro-technology company with a group of academic specialists in neuroscience, biology and robotics in 2016, although it wasn't announced to the press until March the following year. Musk himself had reportedly put $100 million into the company by July 2019.

The publicly stated aim of Neuralink is as follows: 'Neuralink is a team of exceptionally talented people. We are creating the future of brain interfaces: building devices now that will help people with paralysis and inventing new technologies that will expand our abilities, our community, and our world.' The deep details of its works are largely secret, but Neuralink feels like it is delving into the pages of science fiction. Indeed, Neuralink's vision of 'neural lace' – inserting profoundly fine probes into the brain to read, interpret and act upon brain signals – has a conceptual link to the 'neural lace' described in the fictional universe in *The Culture*, a series of sci-fi novels by Iain M. Banks.

The immediate objective for Neuralink is the possibility of helping people with paralysis gain control of computers and electronic devices through brain power alone. (Neuralink has already had success getting a monkey to play video games with its mind.) But Neuralink acknowledges that the 'technology has the potential to treat a wide range of neurological disorders, to restore sensory and movement function, and eventually to expand how we interact with each other, with the world, and with ourselves.' Where this could lead is profound or unnerving, depending on your position (and there have been many scientific critics of the Neuralink work). In an interview with Clubhouse in February 2021, Musk wandered into the realm of possibilities:

The 'you' of a month ago is not the same as the 'you' of today.
I mean a bunch of brain cells have died some memories, some

memories have faded, some have strengthened. There are new memories. So anyway, the point is you wouldn't be. You could, there could be something analogous to a video game, like a saved game situation, where you are able to resume and upload your last state. Yeah. Like in *Altered Carbon* [a sci-fi TV series in which consciousness is transferable]. Maybe lose a few memories but mostly be you, so now that's the long-term stuff. In the short-term stuff for Neuralink the idea would really just be to address brain injuries or spinal injuries and make up for whatever lost capacity somebody has with a chip . . . [an] implanted chip.

The idea of fundamentally integrating memory with technology is eye-widening and raises the greatest of ethical and existential questions. With companies like Neuralink, it seems we are just cracking open a door that might lead into either sunlit vistas or dark alleys. Musk is attempting to ensure that it is the former. In a way, Neuralink offers the potential for humans to plug gaps in their intelligence, performance and consciousness, possibly one day giving us all Musk-like minds.

GETTING EDUCATED

Musk's track record has, if anything, revealed a man who is intensely interested in intelligence, its formulation, expression and practical output. While this interest has taken him into important areas of digital and artificial intelligence, it has also led to explorations of how intelligence is fostered socially, and that means addressing education.

On the whole, Musk is deeply critical of the way that formal education, particularly in the USA, is currently structured and practised. Education is an opportunity to give young people both a passion for learning and, equally, a range of intellectual tools and knowledge sets that will serve them well for the future. For Musk, most standard state and exclusive private education systems fail signally to achieve any of these goals. This failure extends all the way up to college level, with universities charging tens of thousands of dollars every year for an education that often gives the student little cognitive or employment advantage for the future. In typically direct fashion, Musk has attempted to tackle this problem by setting up his own education system.

Before we delve into this school experiment, we can unpack Musk's views on education with more precision. In 2014, at SXSW, Musk was asked what he would do to change the education system. His answer clearly reflects his 'first principles' strategy of thinking through a problem:

> Generally you want education to be as like close to a video game as possible, like a good video game. You do not need to tell your kids to play video games – they will play video games on autopilot all day. So if you can make it interactive and engaging then you can make education far more compelling and far easier to do. So you really want to disconnect the whole grade level thing from the subjects, allow people to progress at the fastest pace that they can […] in each subject. It seems like a really obvious thing.

Musk then went on to say that much schooling today has become little more than presentational, the teacher standing at the front and teaching the same content that they have been offering over several years. Elsewhere, Musk has also expounded a belief that the actual teaching content in schools is too divorced from practical, real-world problem-solving, a tendency that further disconnects the student from study, while also ensuring that the young adults that emerge are not always well equipped to make an impact.

Back at the SXSW event, Musk was then asked whether university was 'unnecessary'. Given that many of his audience had likely spent, or were in the process of spending, tens of thousands of dollars on a college education, his answer cut to the quick:

> A university education is often unnecessary. That's not to say it's unnecessary for all people, but I think you probably learn about as much as you are going to learn there in your first two years, and most of it is from your classmates. Now for a lot of companies they do want to see the completion of the degree, because they are looking for someone who will persevere through to the end, and that's actually what's important to them. But it really depends on what someone's goal is. If they want to start a company, then I would say there's no point in finishing college. It shouldn't be like there are these grades and people move in lock step – and so everyone will normally go through English, Math, Science and so forth, like fifth grade, sixth grade, seventh grade, like it's an assembly line. But people are not objects on an assembly line.

It is relatively easy to see how Musk's personal history might inform his views on education, not least because most of the great leaps forward in Musk's life have been accomplished by doing things in a way that cut against the grain of conventional wisdom, and to a large degree conventional education. He has stated that when hiring his staff, he is more drawn towards the person who has dropped out of college to do something innovative and interesting, rather than someone who has dutifully finished their programme of study. He has also opined that high academic achievement offers no guarantees that it will translate into performance or achievement at work. In a summary sentence in another speech, Musk said that 'We need something new and exciting to latch onto, something that will replace the severely outdated current education system.'

Musk's views on education began to find a low-key outlet in 2014, when he reportedly took his own five children out of their private education and started his own school, known as Ad Astra, Latin for 'To the stars'. Appropriately for its title, the school was founded within the SpaceX building in Hawthorne, California, as a kind of home-schooling project for Musk's children and for those of a select group of SpaceX employees. This was a small group – there were only nine pupils at first – and they were taught by one of the teachers from Musk's children's former school, the inspirational Joshua Dahn, plus one other teacher.

The schooling was provided free, and run on a not-for-profit basis, but Ad Astra was referred to as 'the most exclusive school in the world' in an article in the *Washington Post* published in 2018. The article, and another published at the same time by Ars Technica, revealed just about as many details as were in the public domain – at the time, the only official information about the school was a LinkedIn page. The school had, by 2018, fewer than 50 pupils aged between 7 and 14. According to an IRS Form 990 document, Musk himself was a substantial source of the school's funding – he contributed $475,000 to the school in 2014 and the same in 2015.

The key difference in the way Ad Astra pursued education lay in its orientation to real-world problem-solving. Instead of rigorously dividing the teaching programme into subject tracks (English, history, maths etc.), the students would be given complex multi-layered problems to solve and would have to acquire the skills and knowledge to do so. These problems were generally linked to subjects close to Musk's heart and to what he sees as the properly relevant skills in the modern world. This led to some curriculum design decisions outsiders would find controversial. According to the Ars Technica article, the overriding focus is on science, maths, engineering and, interestingly, ethics. Sports, music and languages were not included, the latter allegedly because Musk believes the computer-aided translation will eventually make the need for language-learning redundant. Another module of curriculum focused on AI – here is doubtless where ethics came into play, given Musk's views on the dangers of the technology. Apparently, the curriculum was (and is) revised every year in response to the previous year's experience and developments in the subject areas, with the students deciding about half of the content for themselves.

But the innovations extended beyond curriculum deep into classroom pedagogy. The statement on the school's initial LinkedIn page was: 'Ad Astra believes in promoting a love of learning, enduring curiosity, and unbounded imagination. Ad Astra is a laboratory school that embraces advancements in the fields of science, technology, and education. [. . .] Ad Astra is dedicated to pushing each student to the frontier of his or her human potential.' The phrase 'laboratory school' here is crucial – Ad Astra's teaching focus was overwhelmingly project-based. Students tackled advanced technological challenges, especially within the 'A-frame' module, which included constructing weather balloons and building fighting robots. Pupils were taught to code in Scheme, Scratch and Swift computer languages, and many also took self-guided courses online. Numerous student-built websites proliferated. Notably, the school also created its own digital currency, to aid the realism of internal trading projects. Each week, the student would have to complete an assignment called Folio, delving into a focused subject in depth. Ars Technica stated: 'One week, it could be the cruise industry, the next, gentrification.' In one exercise, students separated into three groups representing the USA, China and North Korea, then had to engage in nuclear armament negotiations. Dahn told Ars Technica: 'One of the North Korean team members led the world to a nuclear holocaust, essentially. It was a truly impactful moment for that kid.' Everything was hands-on or fully interactive – the fact that the school was located in an actual rocket factory made it the perfect environment to pursue this goal.

Ars Technica described Ad Astra as fostering 'an atmosphere closer to a venture capital incubator than a traditional school', but it is clear that this is exactly what many parents in Silicon Valley wanted for their children. In 2017 (again according to Ars Technica), 400 families competed for just 12 places in the school, admission being screened by the child taking a reasoning test developed by child psychologists. Yet the demand for Ad Astra clearly provided Musk and Dahn with food for further thought, not least how the principles of the school could be extended into the wider public domain, giving others beyond the SpaceX community access to the principles of real-world-centric education.

The awareness of demand led, in 2016, to the foundation of a new online school called Astra Nova, still led by Dahn, focused on students in the particularly formative age bracket of 6 to 14. The key difference between Ad Astra and Astra Nova was, according to Dahn himself: 'Ad Astra was the school at SpaceX that served 50 students; Astra Nova is the online school that aims to reach millions by sharing the insights from our work.'

Astra Nova's lean, super-modern website provides educational content that reflects its vision on adaptive critical thinking. The 'Conundrums' section offers a variety of ethical and intellectual dilemmas, presented as video animations. The first of these, for example, is the 'Blue Comet Conundrum', in which pupils have to decide who gets to name a new, blue comet spotted in the sky – a scientist, a student or an astronaut – based on the back story given to each individual in the presentation. The second major learning zone on the website is 'Synthesis', a collaborative problem-solving class that builds upon the practices established at Ad Astra. The promotional video for Synthesis demonstrates that in a rapidly changing world, 'we believe that kids need to learn how to think for themselves. They need practice in solving complex problems through collaboration and practice making tough decisions in the face of uncertainty.' Through Astra Nova, students get to collaborate online 'with peers and facilitators from around the world [...] Kids compete in teams to solve complex problems that rework the tough decisions that we face in the real world – they build networks, curate art collections, manage ocean ecosystems, control wildfires and colonize space.' The key point of Synthesis is to get the students to 'Practice making tough decisions with others', something the school sees as a factor distinguishing Astra Nova from most other education.

Dahn has been the primary practical and pedagogical driving force behind both Ad Astra and Astra Nova. On the Astra Nova website, it states that the 'only directive from Elon was to "make it great"'. The 2015 IRS filing showed that Musk spent only one hour a week at the school, unsurprising given his massive wider commitments. Yet it seems clear that the school's philosophy is a direct trickle-down from Musk's deeply held beliefs about how to make education relevant to a future that will be profoundly different at every level from the past. We only need to look at Astra Nova's 'Five Axioms of Synthesis' to see their relevance to how Musk has pursued his goals and tackled repeated challenges:

(1) embrace the chaos
(2) test your assumptions
(3) seek good explanations
(4) expect course corrections
(5) contribute to the good.

Astra Nova is, of course, a drop in the ocean in the international education system. Nor is it entirely original – the principles of active learning and project-based real-world thinking have been discussed and developed for many years, with varying degrees of success and distribution. Given Musk's track record of disrupting conventional models and scaling up projects to have a global impact, Astra Nova and its principles may well come to have a far wider impact than we currently see.

CHAPTER 6
THE MUSK MINDSET

The world's self-made billionaires attract the interest of the general public for a variety of reasons – leadership and management skills; financial decision-making; investment portfolio; personal grit and tenacity. Although Elon Musk presents much to discover in each of these categories and many more besides, a substantial part of the public fascination comes down to an abiding interest in the way his mind works. The method by which Musk acquires and synthesizes knowledge is the subject of countless YouTube videos and articles, as the outside world attempts to deduce the secret formula of his prodigious intelligence. There lies the hope that as exceptional as Elon Musk is, there is something in there amounting to a transferable skill.

Musk's exceptionalism in terms of intelligence is not just the veneration of lesser mortals looking in from the sidelines. Almost everyone who makes contact with Musk comes away from the encounter impressed by the dexterity and depth of his brain power. For example, the American billionaire Charlie Munger (vice chairman of Warren Buffet's Berkshire Hathaway conglomerate holding company), a man noted not only for his sharp entrepreneurialism but also his management wisdom, was asked about his impression of Musk in a Q&A at the 2014 Daily Journal Annual Meeting. He replied: 'I think Elon Musk is a genius, and I don't use that word lightly. I think he's also one of the boldest men that ever came down the pike.' Munger's impression of Musk usefully captures the intellectual fuel that has powered the Musk empire, a fusion of acute brainpower with innovative courage.

It is clear that Elon Musk is not 'merely' an entrepreneur. In many ways, the wealth outputs of his ventures are incidental, the necessary outcomes of intelligence applied to practical and engineering problems, rather than the goal of generating more money from existing money (such effort belongs more to the realm of fund managers and venture capitalists). Musk is, fundamentally, an engineer. He has said: 'I guess the way I usually describe myself is an engineer because most of what I do is engineering.' That statement, as we will see, can be applied to almost every corner of Musk's business empire.

THINKING IT THROUGH

Although Musk has not written down his definitive formula for mental performance, he has given enough reflections upon thinking, education, intelligence and problem-solving for us to get a reasonable insight into how he optimizes his mind. The good news indeed is that while Musk recognizes intelligence as partly a composite gift from genetics, nutrition, parenting and other elements over which we have little or no control, there are certain rules of thinking that we can all acquire and apply.

Simplifying, I see Musk's view of intelligence as grounded in the following:

1) The absorption and retention of information
2) The synthesis of ideas and information
3) First principles thinking

4) Resistance to cognitive biases

5) The conversion of ideas into action

Taking the first of these, there is no doubt that Musk is endowed with an exceptional memory, beyond that of even the most adept pub quiz team member. Although the validity of the concept of a 'photographic memory' is one debated by psychologists, it does seem that from his earliest years Musk was able to take a rapid imprint of data and information when they were presented to him. In discussions with Vance, Musk described his highly visual bias for mental processing as a young man, likening his brain to a graphics chip in a computer. Information, problems and solutions came to him as accessible imagery, creating maps of meaning in his head. In 2020, during an interview at the Axel Spring Award, Musk responded to questions about his memory, and whether it was truly photographic in nature. He responded: 'I have a photographic memory in some respects. For technical stuff, I have a very good memory for a human. Computers are much better.' The stand-out phrase in this quotation is 'very good memory for a human', as if Musk is both recognizing that he sits on the upper end of the intelligence scale, but at the same time is perfectly clear about the limitations of brain power in the human species. In a Reddit thread in 2015, Musk was asked by a knowledge-thirsty follower, 'How do you learn so much so fast?' Before giving the answer, to which we shall turn in a moment, Musk was open about the fact that he was not claiming intellectual superman status: 'I do kinda feel like my head is full! My context switching penalty is high and my process isolation is not what it used to be.' Musk here self-analyses using the language of computers. By treating his own brain as a physical system, a product of natural engineering with certain performance and structural characteristics, Musk seems to probe the possibility of compensating for system problems through mental engineering improvements, or ultimately outsourcing intelligence to more robust systems in the digital domain, as we saw in the previous chapter.

In the rest of the Reddit entry quoted on the previous page, Musk does offer a practical insight into how he organizes and retains information in his head, and makes some encouraging noises for the regular public:

> Frankly, though, I think most people can learn a lot more than they think they can. They sell themselves short without trying.
>
> One bit of advice: it is important to view knowledge as sort of a semantic tree – make sure you understand the fundamental principles, ie the trunk and big branches, before you get into the leaves/details or there is nothing for them to hang on to.

Musk's 'semantic tree' has been pored over by business analysts and thinking experts. It is grounded in solid psychological theory and practice. Memories are generated by three fundamental processes: 1) attention – an active concentration directed towards the inputs that need to be remembered; 2) encoding – storing the information in such a way that it moves from the short-term memory to the long-term memory, especially through associating the new inputs with existing knowledge and memories; 3) retrieval – bringing the memories back into consciousness. Musk's idea of the semantic tree powerfully addresses all three elements of memory formation, in a way that is practical and quick to apply.

The semantic tree is essentially a way of organizing information mentally. The trunk of the tree is the core topic being studied, and the subsequent fork and the very largest lower branches are the key subdivisions of that topic. You have to understand all these, simply and sturdily, before anything else can be added; it is pointless spending your thinking time attempting to remember hundreds or thousands of disconnected chunks of information as they flit through your consciousness, as they are not integrated into the network of associations. With the trunk, fork and major boughs secured, in both detail and concept, the thinker can then more successfully add the detailed information of the finer branches and twigs.

Formulating knowledge using this framework, either instinctively or as a deliberate memory device, reinforces the process of both attention and encoding, as the brain actively places all the pieces of information in an associative context, every individual byte of information reinforced by the rest. But the framework also assists retrieval, as the thinker can follow the paths from the trunk upwards, each connection acting as a prompt for recall by association. Using such a system, the whole memory structure then has strong roots.

Of course, Musk may well be speaking of the semantic tree as an analogy rather than a deliberate memory device, but this in no way impairs the effectiveness of principle. Musk is encouraging us to get to grips with fundamental ideas first, then hang the details off this secure framework.

SYNTHESIS

The second part of a putative 'Musk mindset' – the synthesis of ideas and information – refers to the way Musk seems to bring in thinking from many different realms to solve problems with innovation and disruption. And here he has a long-standing but simple advantage – Musk reads a lot, and the right sort of works. The 'leaders are readers' principle has a long and respected back history, and Musk embodies it perfectly. In his childhood, recounted in Chapter 1, Musk voraciously consumed entire shelves of books as if draining them of information. To this day, Musk has maintained the activity of reading informative, interesting and challenging books. Although he reads a wide range of content, his patterns of reading do not seem to be purposeless intellectual wandering. Rather, they are a directed effort to give his semantic tree more associative branches, which in turn gives him more base material with which to make informed decisions and connected innovations.

Musk has revealed an ever-evolving shortlist of the titles that have been particularly important to his thinking, or which he has publicly recommended. A selection of these titles includes:

1. The science fiction works of Isaac Asimov and Robert Heinlein
2. J.R.R. Tolkien, *Lord of the Rings* (1954–55)
3. Frank Herbert, *Dune* (1965)
4. Ayn Rand, *Atlas Shrugged* (1996)
5. J.E. Gordon, *Structures: Or Why Things Don't Fall Down* (2003)
6. Nick Bostrom, *Superintelligence: Paths, Dangers, Strategies* (2014)
7. Max Tegmark, *Life 3.0: Being Human in the Age of Artificial Intelligence* (2017)

8. Ian Goodfellow, Yoshua Bengio and Aaron Courville, *Deep Learning* (2016)

9. Naomi Oreskes and Erik M. Conway, *Merchants of Doubt: How a Handful of Scientists Obscured the Truth on Issues from Tobacco Smoke to Climate Change* (2010)

10. Sean Carroll, *The Big Picture: On the Origins of Life, Meaning, and the Universe Itself* (2017)

11. Sam Harris, *Lying* (2013)

12. Adam Smith, *The Wealth of Nations* (1776)

13. Walter Isaacson, *Benjamin Franklin: An American Life* (2004) and *Einstein: His Life and Universe* (2008)

14. Donald L. Barlett and James B. Steele, *Howard Hughes: His Life and Madness* (2004)

15. Robert K. Massie, *Catherine the Great: Portrait of a Woman* (2011)

16. Richard Branson, *Screw Business as Usual: Turning Capitalism into a Force for Good* (2017)

17. Peter Thiel, *Zero to One: Notes on Startups, or How to Build the Future* (2014)

This list is just the thinnest of slices from hundreds of works that Musk has read over his lifetime, but it gives a measure of insight into the types of information and thinking to which he gravitates. They break down into certain logical categories. Science fiction and fantasy novels are common on the shelves of tech entrepreneurs, being genres with an obvious attraction for those fascinated by futurity. But Musk ranges more widely and freely across the non-fiction spectrum, from philosophy and science across to biographies and business management. While this might, at first glance, appear to be an indicator of a flitting mind, seen holistically, Musk's reading habits are far more to do with intellectual syncretism, merging different fields of study into a unified whole, each topic feeding into the other.

Some titles from Musk's reading list certainly come across as more central to his life experience than others. In an interview with Alison van Diggelen on 22 January 2013 at the Computer History Museum, for example, he explained how one title in particular, read while he was still a boy, opened up some critical philosophical and logical vistas for him.

I guess when I was around 12 or 15 ... I had an existential crisis, and I was reading various books on trying to figure out the meaning of life and what does it all mean? It all seemed quite meaningless and then we happened to have some books by Nietzsche and Schopenhauer in the house, which you should not read at age 14 (laughter). It is bad, it's really negative. So then I read *Hitchhiker's Guide to the Galaxy* which is quite positive I think and it highlighted an important point which is that a lot of times the question is harder than the answer. And if you can properly phrase the question, then the answer is the easy part. So, to the degree that we can better understand the universe, then we can better know what questions to ask. Then whatever the question is that most approximates: what's the meaning of life? That's the question we can ultimately get closer to understanding. And so I thought to the degree that we can expand the scope and scale of consciousness and knowledge, then that would be a good thing.

Musk is far from the first tech entrepreneur to be influenced by *The Hitchhiker's Guide to the Galaxy*. The point he makes about the importance of questions, however, still seems relevant to his way of thinking. The questions we ask, and particularly the clarity with which we frame them, are engines for generating ideas and forward momentum. For Musk, ideas on the page are not frozen there – he takes written concepts, facts, beliefs, data and more and then activates them in reality, something also proven to be cement information firmly in the memory. His reading is, above all, pragmatic. We can see this in some very direct instances. For example, at the conceptual stages of SpaceX, Jim Cantrell lent Musk several key textbooks, including: *Rocket Propulsion Elements* (2010), *Aerothermodynamics of Gas Turbine and Rocket Propulsion* (1996), *Fundamentals of Astrodynamics* (1971) and the *International Reference Guide to Space Launch Systems* (2004). Cantrell has publicly stated his amazement at the way Musk committed the information from these titles to memory, being able to recount lengthy passages verbatim. So, Musk literally taught himself rocket science.

But Cantrell has also explained that Musk does not overestimate his capabilities for mastering any given subject, regardless of his formidable powers of knowledge acquisition. He notes that Musk is equally attentive to expert people, spending time with or hiring the best representatives in relevant fields. Cantrell observed that when Musk was in the company of experts, he would give them his fullest attention: 'It was as if he would suck the experience out of them. He truly listens to people.'

Musk's ability to direct absolute attention to what he is studying or the people he is talking to is imperative to understanding his accelerated learning. Strong attention anchors the first two elements of memory formation – encoding and storage – and thereby lays firm foundations for the final retrieval stage. For Musk, the semantic tree is strengthened by the way its branches are united in a purposeful trunk. Reflecting on his reading of Isaacson's biography of Benjamin Franklin, Musk mused (in an interview for CNN) that: 'I think in the case of Franklin he did what needed to be done at the time it needed to be done. So he was in different fields and he thought about what was the most important thing that needed to be accomplished right now and he worked on that.' Like Musk, Franklin was a true polymath – he was a writer, printer and publisher, a political philosopher, a scientist and inventor, a statesman and diplomat, one of the Founding Fathers of the USA (most famously a drafter and signer of the Declaration of Independence), the first US postmaster general, the first US ambassador to France and president of the state of Pennsylvania. But Musk recognizes that there is a world of difference between knowing something and getting something done with that knowledge. To make that transition, the mental library of knowledge and skills needs directing into a purposeful and focused endeavour.

Musk is a disruptor by nature. On a Quora post, Cantrell was asked the provocative question, 'Is Elon Musk a visionary or just a crazy man?' The opening to his response stepped outside the interrogative framework:

He's actually neither in my opinion – he's a Rogue. He has some very grandiose visions: make 'Mankind a multi-planetary species' and to 'remove humanity's dependence on fossil fuels' to which he applies enormous energy, time and resources. Elon is very intelligent, has a nearly inexhaustible energy, and possesses an incredible appetite for making progress. He is really a Rogue because he does it outside of the normal channels of thinking and outside of the normal channels of doing. He, like many of us who have joined him at various parts of his adventures, simply realized at a point in our lives that radical transformation cannot happen within the system but must happen from outside the system. Some of us even believe that the larger economic system and society actually hinders progress and you have to be on the outside of it to truly change things for the better.

Here, Cantrell persuasively makes his case for the 'Rogue' interpretation of Musk's character. What could appear to be the vaunting ambitions of a man unchained from reality are in reality the hyper-pragmatic ambitions of a man defying conventional thinking and attempting 'radical transformation'. This angle on life is surely also a key ingredient in Musk's mental ability. Memory and innovation are both strengthened by stepping outside standard models, an act that reinforces the ownership of thinking, rather than simply wearing a deeper groove in well-worn paths.

FIRST PRINCIPLES

This leads us to another cornerstone of Musk's mental gymnastics, what he calls reasoning from first principles. Here, Musk encourages us to free ourselves from conformity to simply reworking existing trends of thought, and instead go back to understanding the groundwork on which the whole discussion rests and then innovating and problem-solving from that basis. It is again, in many ways, a reflection of the semantic tree theory, the thinker laying the roots and growing a robust trunk of understanding before adding the sophisticated superstructure of boughs and branches. What is important, however, is that the thinker ditches much of the baggage of existing knowledge before thinking the issue through.

Musk explained thinking via first principles in an interview with Kevin Rose for Innominds:

> I think it is also important to reason from first principles rather than by analogy. The normal way we conduct our lives is that we reason by analogy. We are doing this because it is like something else that is being done, or it's like what other people are doing. It's like iterations on a theme. It's mentally easier to reason by analogy than by first principles. First principles is kind of a physics principle of looking at the world. And what it means is that you boil things down to the most fundamental truths. We say, 'What are we sure is true, or as sure as possible is true?' And then we reason up from there. And that takes a lot more mental energy.

What is perhaps most interesting in this passage is the summary statement about first principles thinking requiring less mental energy than reasoning by analogy. He does not specifically explain why it should be less mentally taxing, but I might suggest that it frees that mind from constantly wrestling to struggling to integrate the knowledge and information of others. There is also the possibility that reasoning by first principles is more motivating and exciting, which in turn produces more mental stamina.

In an important interview with Lex Fridman in December 2021,

Musk went deeper into first principles thinking. He connected it explicitly with physics, stating that 'Physics is law and every other thing is suggestion. Anyone can break the law but no one can break physics.' He grounded this statement by explaining that first principles thinking can be applied to all manner of life problems, not just scientific ones, but the crucial point was that you define the fundamental realities of the situation – 'the things that we are most confident are true' – and then sit subsequent thinking atop this platform, 'setting your axiomatic base'. Any conclusions derived thereafter have to be cross-checked against the foundations that have been established.

In his aforementioned interview with Kevin Rose, Musk gives an example to demonstrate this approach to critical thinking. He looks specifically at battery technology. In his view, the conventional thinking about battery packs is that they are, of necessity, both heavy and expensive, costing about $600 per kilowatt hour of energy. Because that's how batteries have been in the past, that's how they will be in the future. Musk calls this thinking 'pretty dumb' and argues that this line of reasoning will never result in turning the wheel in a new direction. Instead, he advocates going back to first principles with a set of simple but directed questions:

> What are the material constituents of the batteries? What is the spot market value of the constituents? So you can say, it's got cobalt, nickel, aluminum, carbon and some polymers for separation, and a steel can. So break that down on a material basis and say OK, if we bought that on a metal exchange what would each of those things cost? It's like, oh, geez, it's like $80 per kilowatt hour. So clearly you just need to think of clever ways to take those materials

and combine them into the shape of a battery cell and you can have batteries that are much, much cheaper than anyone realised.

Going back to the Fridman interview, we see Musk add another nuance to his strategy for breaking problems down into fundamental concepts. He explained how 'another good physics tool is thinking of things in the limit'. In this methodology, Musk talks about seeing how the problem shifts in nature when you scale it up to a very small number or a very large number. In manufacturing, for example, the cost models change radically depending on whether you are producing single-digits units or whether you are producing millions of units – scaling in either direction can reveal what needs to be done to reach the requisite efficiencies of time and cost.

COGNITIVE BIASES

By all accounts of former employees, being under the hot lamp of Elon Musk's questioning can be a deeply uncomfortable experience. On any matter, be it an engineering challenge or a point of financial management, Musk will ruthlessly squirrel into the heart of the issue through relentless and close questioning, until he feels satisfied that he has reached either clarity or a solution. Woolly or imprecise thinking can generate a heated response, particularly in relation to issues that are fundamental to the efficiency and realization of the project vision. Musk's interrogations apparently take little account of the personal feelings of those facing the logical barrage. All that matters is the answer. Ryan Popple, an ex-US Army man appointed as Tesla's director of finance, explained of Musk's presence in the company during the tumultuous times of the late 2000s: 'If you started falling behind there was hell to pay. Everyone could see it, and people lost their jobs when they didn't deliver. Elon has a mind that's a bit like a calculator. If you put a number on the projector that does not make sense, he will spot it. He doesn't miss details' (quoted in Vance 2015: 182). Employees have also noted, however, that if under interrogation the responder holds up their side of the equation and provides relevant details and new information that have merit, then Musk might indeed change his mind and direction – what matters to Musk is the answer, not the ego. (He has said that it is actually vital to elicit critical feedback, 'particularly from friends', as the latter will hopefully combine honesty with having your best interests at heart.)

A context for Musk's unwavering commitment to extracting the best thinking from his employees is a tweet he posted on 19 December 2021, simply: 'Should be taught to all at a young age'. He followed this statement with a graphic, produced by TitleMax, headed: '50 Cognitive Biases to be Aware of so You Can be the Very Best Version of You'. The graphic lists, with short examples of each, 50 fundamental errors in thinking. They included elements such as: 'Self-Serving Bias', in which we take credit for our successes but not for our failures; 'Curse of Knowledge', where we assume that everyone knows what we do; 'Google Effect (aka Digital Amnesia)' – we quickly forget information that we look up online; 'Authority Bias', in which we are unduly influenced by authority figures without testing their theories; and 'Blind Spot Bias', where we think bias is only for other people, not for ourselves.

The full list (a link is provided in the Bibliography) is well worth the study time, as it exposes the mind's deep internal wrestle between truth and error, with many ingrained tendencies trying to steer us towards the latter. During his interview with Lex Fridman,

Musk gave a more scientifically nuanced view of the operating system running inside our minds:

> We currently operate on two layers. We have a limbic, like primitive brain layer, which is [where] all of our impulses come from. [. . .] We've got like a monkey brain with a computer stuck on it. That's the human brain. And a lot of our impulses and everything are driven by the monkey brain. And the computer of the cortex is constantly trying to make the monkey brain happy. It's not the cortex that's steering the monkey brain, it's the monkey brain steering the cortex. [. . .] Surely the really smart thing should control the dumb thing, but actually the dumb thing controls the smart thing.

The conversation went on to Musk reflecting on developing a 'tertiary layer' of intelligence, the digital super-intelligence discussed in the previous chapter. Sticking with biological potentiality, however, it is clear that Musk does not see human beings as operating purely within the tidy boundaries of reason. 'The natural human tendency is for wishful thinking,' he has stated.

While Musk would never claim to have freed himself from either cognitive biases or the limbic system, he has repeatedly demonstrated a pattern of mental non-conformity. He has said in interview how his study of physics in particular has been useful in sharpening his thinking, as it teaches the students to go back to the first principles outlined above and follow the scientific framework rigorously until the thinker gets as close to truth as possible. The framework even holds good when thinking about the most counterintuitive elements of physics (Musk references quantum mechanics as an example – https://www.youtube.com/watch?v=5mtGdIsHxyU), the method by its nature providing a counterbalance to the cognitive biases you might automatically bring to such problems.

Musk has also advocated a general investment in good critical thinking processes. 'Just in general, critical thinking is good. You know, examining whether you have the correct axioms, or the most applicable axioms. Does the logic necessarily connect? And then, what are the range of probable outcomes? Outcomes are usually not deterministic but they are a range. And so you want to figure out what those probabilities are [to] make sure ideally that you are the house. [...] It's fine to gamble as long as you are the house'. This last statement is a pithy frame to put around much of Musk's career, which has typically involved gambling to an extent that would induce a heart attack in most of us. The logical method, in essence, is the house, the 'computer of the cortex', a locus of control that can reduce (never remove) the risk from the roulette wheel while also protecting the self from the primitive drives and impulses that might cause us to act in ways that are not in our best interests.

Musk also seems to apply his models of critical thinking to the hiring process. As we have seen throughout this book, Musk and his companies gravitate towards super-bright people with slightly maverick tendencies. They also prize individuals who have the practicality and youthful energy to get things done without the lazy warmth that can be generated by a big corporate structure, accustomed to more stratified and documented working methods. One element Musk lasers in on during recruitment and interviewing is demonstrable proof that the individual is capable of: a) solving problems with creativity and innovation; and b) can get things done. On 6 November 2020, Musk tweeted to his 'Muskateers': 'When sending your resumé, please describe a few of the hardest problems you solved & exactly how you solved them.' The request in some ways appears simple, but it has hidden sophistications. It bypasses the focus on qualifications to reframe thinking on process and achievement. It also cuts through the self-laudatory padding that often gathers on CVs – to Musk, it doesn't matter what you feel about yourself, it only matters how you think and what you can do. 'Be rigorous in your self-analysis' is another pertinent Muskian piece of wisdom.

THE BIAS FOR ACTION

Of course, the world is replete with academically intelligent people who have never achieved even a fraction of 1 per cent of what Elon Musk has in his five-plus decades on this planet. In one interview, Musk was asked directly what it is that separates him from other brilliant engineers or very capable managers, in terms of the immense qualitative and quantitative difference in achievements. The question brought something of an awkward and hesitant moment of reflection on Musk's part, almost as if the question wasn't really relevant to the way he sees the world. But when an answer haltingly emerged, it was revelatory, with a touch of humour and realism:

First of all, I certainly don't think that I can do anything or that I can do most things that people think are impossible – a lot of what people think is impossible is actually impossible. But occasionally it's not. [. . .] Really believe in what you are doing, but not just from a blind faith standpoint, but to have really thought about it and said 'OK, this is true, I'm convinced it's true. I've tried every angle to figure out if it's untrue and sought negative feedback to figure out maybe if I'm wrong. But after all that it still seems like this is the right way to go. I think that gives one a fundamental conviction and an ability to convey that conviction to others.

Musk's opening lines here push back against the 'believe you can achieve the impossible' mantras that characterize the more optimistic strands of Western business self-help. Musk believes that humanity has a natural leaning towards wishful thinking, and just the act of believing you can do something does not always make reality conform. What is far more powerful, Musk here outlines, is to have a truly compelling idea that motivates you at every level, *including cognitively*. It is this intellectual part that is often missing from many motivational addresses. Musk finds motivation in a good idea *after* it has been rigorously tested and analysed and still seems to hold its potential and value following pressure testing. Of course, this does not remove risk, a factor to which Musk has confessed he has a 'high tolerance', but in many ways his achievements are precisely matched with his logically considered ideas.

Seen through this lens, Musk's legendary capacity for working super-human hours becomes perhaps a little more understandable. The idea provides its own energy and drive. After that, things get a bit more basic – be 'extremely tenacious, and then just work like hell, I mean you have to put in 80–100-hour weeks, every week'. Musk certainly has, in unbeatable volumes, what we might term 'grit'. Vance quotes Antonio Gracias, the founder and CEO of Valor Equity, who witnessed Musk at the full peak of stress management in 2008.

Gracias explained that in his view the experience Musk went through in 2008 'would have broken anyone else'. Yet he witnessed Musk digging into impressive reserves of focus, attaining a 'hyperrational' state that gave him exceptional powers of long-term decision-making even when under continual and exhausting pressures. In Gracias's view, this quality is one characteristic that truly separates Musk from many other executives within his company and many other competitors without. He can withstand levels of intellectual pain and mental discomfort that few others can, with Gracias noting that Musk's cognitive ability seems to increase in power in inverse proportion to the pressures placed upon him – 'The harder it gets, the better he gets' (Vance 2015: 214).

Such a quality is a rarity in any field of endeavour. Perhaps the only hint of why Musk is able to achieve this is the reference to his becoming 'hyperrational'. It is certainly the case that the greatest enemy of a successful outcome to a stressful situation is panic; Musk maybe simply gets that fact, and realizes logic and application offer the best exits.

The idea that long working hours equates to productivity has been questioned over recent years by leading economists and academics specializing in workplace practices. For example, a productivity study by Stanford and Institute for the Study of Labor (IZA) economics professor John Pencavel in 2014 found that productivity per hour dipped significantly after 50 hours per week and after 55 hours, the productivity drops off so much that any extra hours contribute almost nothing to the weekly output (although this study was focused on manual workers). Similarly, a study of consultants by Erin Reid, a professor at Boston University's Questrom School of Business, discovered that by and large, senior management could not distinguish the productivity outputs between those consultants who worked 80 hours per week and those who merely pretended to do so.

In the case of Musk, however, he does appear to have an elevated capacity to push himself to work longer hours with genuine productivity. He has proven this not just in nebulous management challenges, the type that offer frequent opportunities to burn away time without overly intensive work, but in hardened engineering work, such as writing software code through the night or working several days straight on the workshop floor at SpaceX to get a job done. Musk has certainly seemed at times less than sympathetic towards those who aspire to more balance between work life and home life. One Tesla employee, for example, told Vance that Musk berated him for taking time off to be present at the birth of his child. Allegedly, Musk said in an email: 'We're changing the world and changing history, and you either commit or you don't' (Vance 2015: 182). (Vance acknowledges in a footnote that he did not see the email personally.)

The combination of a superb functional intelligence, high motivation behind a proven idea, an elevated tolerance of risk and the ability to work with Herculean endurance are key characteristics behind Musk's success. There have been recent signs that Musk might be conceding some ground to the effects of age, however. In August 2018, Musk gave an interview to the *New York Times* in which he appeared to confess to some of the symptoms of corporate burn-out. He reflected upon the fact that he hadn't taken more than a week off work since 2001, that recently he had been doing 120-hour weeks (on occasions he would spend three or four days within his factory facilities without leaving or going outside), and that on the night of his 47th birthday he worked for 24 hours straight, and that his sleeping was affected, requiring him to take Ambien (sleep medication). (The Tesla stock price fell by as much as 8 per cent on the day following publication of the interview.)

While some might say that Musk's admissions were signs that he is slowing down, I would argue that the implications are rather different. Musk, to my knowledge, while accepting he has certain heightened abilities, has never claimed that he is any sort of superhuman. Indeed, Musk is perfectly aware of the 'flaws' in the system of every human being. What ultimately matters to Musk is following the logic, however it presents itself.

CONCLUSION

Elon Musk is a figure of controversy, of that there is no doubt. Slip a bookmark into almost any chapter of his life and there will be some personal Musk story or incident that absorbed as many column inches as his business exploits. His intimate life has been under particularly microscopic evaluation. His marriage to Talulah Riley ended in divorce in 2012, then remarriage in 2013, then a final divorce in 2016. He subsequently dated the Hollywood actress Amber Heard in 2017. This relationship became entwined in the media through Heard's subsequent, and disastrous, marriage to the actor Johnny Depp, the latter in court proceedings accusing Heard and Musk of having an affair during the marriage, an accusation Heard flatly denied. In 2018, Musk began dating the Canadian musician Grimes, and they bore a son in May 2020, named 'X AE A-XII' (pronounced, according to interviews with Musk and Grimes, as 'Ex Ash A Twelve' or 'Ex Ay Eye). They also have a daughter, Exa Dark Sideræl Musk, born in December 2021 via a surrogate. The couple subsequently, and amicably, separated. At the time of writing, there have also been press reports that in 2021 Musk fathered twins with Shivon Zilis, an executive from Neuralink.

The media's magnetism towards the personal relationships of celebrity is long-standing. Musk has provided them with other ingredients for consumption. In classical terminology, we might view him as an eccentric. He has appeared in minor parts on

As his wealth and success have grown, the media has taken ever deeper interest in Musk's personal life, and especially his romantic relationships. Here he is seen with the musician, singer, songwriter and record producer Grimes at the 2018 Met Gala, held at the Metropolitan Museum of Art in New York.

Another notable foray into acting – Elon Musk plays himself in 'The Platonic Permutation', a November 2015 episode of the popular network show The Big Bang Theory.

screen, such as the films *Iron Man 2* (2010), *Why Him?* (2016) and *Men in Black: International* (2019), and several TV series, including *The Simpsons*, *The Big Bang Theory*, *South Park* and (with more gravitas) in the Netflix documentary *Return to Space*. Musk even hosted the Mother's Day 2021 episode of *Saturday Night Live* (*SNL*), in which his mother also made an appearance. (Her most memorable line: 'I'm excited for my Mother's Day gift. I just hope it's not dogecoin.') For good measure, Musk has written and released and partly performed two music tracks, one a rap ('RIP Harambe') and the other for the electronic dance music (EDM) genre ('Don't Doubt Ur Vibe').

In December 2019, a new, severe respiratory virus was detected in the city of Wuhan, Hubei Province, China. By the spring of 2020, what we now know as Covid-19 had spread globally, beginning a pandemic that plunged the world into the worst social crisis since the Second World War. Entire nations were plunged into

A true indicator of Elon Musk's celebrity status was his guest hosting of Saturday Night Live *on 8 May 2021. He acted in several sketches, here alongside (L–R, omitting Musk) Mikey Day, Chris Redd and Melissa Villaseñor during the 'Chad on Mars' sketch.*

law-enforced lockdowns of varying severity. Hospitals creaked and failed under the avalanche of Covid cases. Pharmaceutical companies raced, and succeeded, to develop new vaccines with unheard-off acceleration. Culturally, there was violent debate over the right way to handle the disease, and indeed disagreement as to what level of threat it presented, and whether chosen responses were proportionate or not.

In September 2020, Elon Musk appeared on the Joe Rogan podcast. The meeting of the two men naturally generated high expectations, not least because of Rogan's undoubted talent in getting his guests to relax and express views, over the prolonged discussion, that they might not otherwise voice. The interview certainly didn't disappoint and is recommended viewing/listening for those wanting an enjoyable unfolding and at times intimate insight into Musk's personality and his views on life and work. It also brought the moment when Musk took a single drag on a cigar, which Rogan claimed was laced with cannabis, an act that appeared to drop the price of Tesla stock by a few points the next day. (Musk flatly denied he was a pot smoker in a subsequent *60 Minutes* interview.)

One interesting moment came when Rogan asked Musk about his opinions on the Covid-19 lockdown policies (the pandemic was raging at its height at this time). He questioned Musk about whether he agreed with those who argued that people should be allowed to go back out and work or whether the continued lockdown should be enforced. Musk's reply forms a useful initial step for moving this biography towards a close:

> My opinion is that if someone wants to stay at home, they should stay at home, and if someone doesn't want to stay at home, they should not be compelled to stay at home. That's my opinion. [. . .] This notion though that you can just sort of send cheques out to everybody and it will be fine is not true, obviously. Some people have this absurd view that the economy is like some magic horn of plenty, like it just makes stuff. There's a magic horn of plenty and the goods and services just come from this magic horn of plenty, and then if somebody has more stuff then somebody else [says] 'They just took more from this magic horn of plenty.' Now let me just break it to the fools out there. *If you don't make stuff, there is no stuff.* [. . .] We've become detached from reality. You can't just legislate money and solve these things. *If you don't make stuff, there is no stuff.*

We can extract two points from this dialogue, connected but also standalone. The first is that Musk's views on the lockdown added fuel to an already roaring fire. Musk was already deep in disputation over his stance on Covid-19. On 13 March 2021, for example, *Forbes* magazine published an article with a loaded title: 'Elon Musk's False Covid Predictions: A Timeline'. Among the examples given were a tweet (6 March 2020) in which Musk stated that 'the coronavirus panic is dumb'; another in which he predicted 'zero new cases' by the end of April 2020); an announcement (11 May 2020) that 'Tesla is restarting production today against Alameda County rules. I will be on the line with everyone else. If anyone is arrested, I ask that it only be me'; and raising some questions about the safety of the vaccines. This author will not plunge into the deep and turbulent waters of the rights and wrongs of Musk's Covid-19 viewpoints. From his interview, however, we can perhaps sense why Musk might instinctively resist the lockdowns and public reactions. Quite simply, *we have to make stuff*. Musk is essentially a realist, and no amount of wishful thinking can get away from the hard facts of production and consumption, and how necessary they are for a society to thrive and grow. Looking across Musk's portfolio, he is very much about stuff – spaceships, cars, boring machines, batteries. He also has a high risk threshold. In April 2021, he tweeted: 'To be clear, I do support vaccines in general & covid vaccines specifically. The science is unequivocal.' But he widened the discussion in the *Time* Person of the Year article in December 2021, when he gave his thoughts about those who chose to go unvaccinated: 'You are taking a risk, but people do risky things all the time. I believe we've got to watch out for the erosion of freedom in America.' For Musk, the social and political freedom to pursue one's goals is paramount in a healthy society, and he is cautious about the potentially widening justifications for curtailing freedoms.

Perhaps the greatest of Musk's controversies came in July and August 2018, when he was in a spat with Vernon Unsworth, a British diver living in Thailand, who assisted in the globally publicized rescue of 12 boys from the water-filled Tham Luang Nang Non cave in Chiang Rai Province, northern Thailand. Unsworth criticized the responsive efforts of Musk and The Boring Company to develop a mini rescue submarine, saying it was just a 'publicity stunt', and the counteraccusations began. Most damaging was Musk's taunt that Unsworth was a 'pedo guy' and, following this, 'You don't think it's strange he hasn't sued me?' The affair escalated into Unsworth launching a defamation case against Musk in December 2019, seeking $190 million in damages. Musk apologized, but was also found not liable for damages, having explained that some of his taunts were just boilerplate hard language from his childhood in South Africa.

Taken together, the controversies surrounding Musk can be a deal-breaker for some people. But I go back to our introduction, and *Time*'s defence of Musk as Person of the Year. Whatever you think of Musk, there is surely no argument about the monumental scale of what he has achieved in his lifetime. During his appearance on *SNL*, Musk revealed that he has Asperger's Syndrome. This condition (more correctly termed autism spectrum disorder) has to be given some weighting in our evaluation of his life and work, both in terms of how his mind operates but also in what he has had to negotiate to achieve greatness. In this biography, we have repeatedly seen a man following logic, risk and ambition wherever they take him, along the way acquiring the knowledge and doing the work to get the job done. As things stand, a significant part of all our futures could in some way be connected to the achievements of Elon Musk.

BIBLIOGRAPHY

BOOKS AND ARTICLES

Ars Staff (25 June 2018). 'First space, then auto—now Elon Musk quietly tinkers with education'. *Arstechnica.com*: https://arstechnica.com/science/2018/06/first-space-then-auto-now-elon-musk-quietly-tinkers-with-education/?amp=1&__twitter_impression=true

Ball, Molly and Jeffrey Kluger, Alejandro de la Garza (13 December 2019). '*Time* 2021 Person of the Year: Elon Musk'. *Time.com*: https://time.com/person-of-the-year-2021-elon-musk/

Berger, Eric (12 January 2019). 'SpaceX cutting 10 percent of its staff to become a leaner company'. *Arstechnica.com*: https://arstechnica.com/science/2019/01/spacex-cutting-10-percent-of-its-staff-to-become-a-leaner-company/

Bryan, Judy (7 April 1998). 'CitySearch, Zip2 Join Forces'. *Wired.com*: https://www.wired.com/1998/04/citysearch-zip2-join-forces/

Caboz, Jay (2 July 2015). 'How To Raise A Billionaire: An Interview With Elon Musk's Father, Errol Musk'. *Forbes.com*: https://www.forbes.com/sites/kerryadolan/2015/07/02/how-to-raise-a-billionaire-an-interview-with-elon-musks-father-errol-musk/?sh=362f2ad57483

Fehrenbacher, Katie (11 June 2019). 'Tesla Founder Eberhard Files Lawsuit Against Tesla, Elon Musk'. *Gigaom.com* (no longer online)

Foust, Jeff (14 November 2005). 'Big Plans for SpaceX'. *The Space Review*: https://www.thespacereview.com/article/497/1

Gelles, David et al. (16 August 2018) 'Elon Musk Details "Excruciating" Personal Toll of Tesla Turmoil'. *NYTimes.com*:

https://www.nytimes.com/2018/08/16/business/elon-musk-interview-tesla.html

Hallman, Carly (accessed 19 April 2022). '50 Cognitive Biases to be Aware of so You Can be the Very Best Version of You'. *Titlemax.com*: https://www.titlemax.com/discovery-center/lifestyle/50-cognitive-biases-to-be-aware-of-so-you-can-be-the-very-best-version-of-you/

Hals, Tom (18 January 2022). 'Tesla investors urge judge to order Musk repay $13 bln for SolarCity deal'. *Reuters.com*: https://www.reuters.com/business/telsa-investors-urge-judge-order-musk-repay-13-bln-solarcity-deal-2022-01-18/

Hanley, Steve (9 July 2016). 'Tesla spends just $6 per car in advertising'. *Teslerati.com*: https://www.teslarati.com/tesla-spends-just-6-per-car-advertising/

Higgins, Tim (2021). *Power Play: Elon Musk, Tesla and the Bet of the Century*. London. Penguin Random House.

Hoffman, Carl (22 May 2007). 'Elon Musk Is Betting His Fortune on a Mission Beyond Earth's Orbit'. *Wired.com*: https://www.wired.com/2007/05/ff-space-musk/?currentPage=all

Holley, Peter (27 June 2018). 'Elon Musk created a secretive "laboratory school" for brilliant kids who love flamethrowers'. *Washingtonpost.com*: https://www.washingtonpost.com/technology/2018/06/27/elon-musk-created-secretive-laboratory-school-brilliant-kids-who-love-flamethrowers/

Hull, Dana (23 June 2021). 'Tesla's Solar Roof Rollout Is a Bust – And a Fixation for Elon Musk'. *Bloomberg.com*: https://www.bloomberg.com/news/articles/2021-06-23/tesla-s-solar-roof-rollout-is-a-bust-and-a-fixation-for-elon-musk

Kanellos, Michael (20 July 2006). 'Electric sports car packs a punch, but will it sell?' *Cnet.com*: https://www.cnet.com/roadshow/news/electric-sports-car-packs-a-punch-but-will-it-sell/

Keats, Robin (2013). 'Rocket man'. *Queen's Alumni Review*: https://www.queensu.ca/gazette/alumnireview/stories/rocket-man

Kiely, Kathy (22 May 2012). 'SpaceX blasts off literally and politically'. *Sunlightfoundation.com*: https://sunlightfoundation.com/2012/05/22/spacex-blasts-literally-and-politically/

Knowledge at Wharton Staff (13 May 2009). 'Harnessing the Sun and Outer Space: Elon Musk's Sky-high Vision'. *Knowledge at Wharton*: https://knowledge.wharton.upenn.edu/article/harnessing-the-sun-and-outer-space-elon-musks-sky-high-vision/

LaMonica, Martin (21 September 2009). 'Tesla Motors founders: Now there are five'. *Cnet.com*: https://www.cnet.com/culture/tesla-motors-founders-now-there-are-five/

Markoff, John (13 December 2015). 'Silicon Valley investors to bankroll artificial-intelligence center'. *Seattletimes.com*: https://www.seattletimes.com/business/technology/silicon-valley-investors-to-bankroll-artificial-intelligence-center/

Marshall, Aarian (14 December 2017). 'Elon Musk Reveals His Awkward Dislike of Mass Transit'. *Wired.com*: https://www.wired.com/story/elon-musk-awkward-dislike-mass-transit/

Matousek, Mark (7 February 2018). 'Tesla created the world's best car commercial without spending a dime on advertising'. *Businessinsider.com*: https://www.businessinsider.com/tesla-made-the-worlds-best-car-commercial-without-spending-money-2018-2?r=US&IR=T

Musk, Justine (10 September 2010). '"I Was a Starter Wife": Inside America's Messiest Divorce'. *Marieclaire.com*: https://www.marieclaire.com/sex-love/a5380/millionaire-starter-wife/

Musk, Maye (2019). *A Woman Makes a Plan: Advice for a Lifetime of Adventure, Beauty, and Success*. New York, Penguin.

Reid, Erin (28 April 2015). 'Why Some Men Pretend to Work 80-Hour Weeks'. *Hbr.org*: https://hbr.org/2015/04/why-some-men-pretend-to-work-80-hour-weeks

Roumeliotis, Greg, and Uday Sampath Kumar, Chavi Mehta (15 April 2022). 'Musk makes $43 billion offer for Twitter to build "arena for free speech"'. *Reuters.com*: https://www.reuters.com/technology/elon-musk-offers-buy-twitter-5420-per-share-2022-04-14/

Sahan, Zachary (26 August 2021). 'Tesla Model 3 Has Passed 1 Million Sales'. *Cleantechnica.com*: https://cleantechnica.com/2021/08/26/tesla-model-3-has-passed-1-million-sales/

Soni, Jimmy (2022). *The Founders: Elon Musk, Peter Thiel, and the Company that Made the Modern Internet – The Inside Story of PayPal*. London, Atlantic Books.

SpaceRef (25 September 2001). 'MarsNow 1.9 Profile: Elon Musk, Life to Mars Foundation'. *SpaceRef.com*: http://www.spaceref.com/news/viewsr.html?pid=3698

Stempel, Jonathan (5 November 2019). 'Tesla settles with Walmart over solar panel installations, fires'. *Reuters.com*: https://www.reuters.com/article/us-walmart-tesla-solar-lawsuit-idUSKBN1XF240

Strauss, Neil (15 November 2017). 'Elon Musk: The Architect of Tomorrow'. *Rollingstone.com*: https://www.rollingstone.com/culture/culture-features/elon-musk-the-architect-of-tomorrow-120850/

Vance, Ashlee (2015). *Elon Musk: How the Billionaire CEO of SpaceX and Tesla is Shaping Our Future*. London, Virgin.

Vance, Ashlee (14 May 2015). 'Elon Musk's Space Dream Almost Killed Tesla'. *Bloomberg.com*: https://www.bloomberg.com/graphics/2015-elon-musk-spacex/

Wnek, Mark (8 February 2018). 'There's Advertising and Marketing, and Then There's Elon Musk'. *Ad Age*. https://adage.com/article/special-report-super-bowl/advertising-marketing-elon-musk/312307

SOCIAL MEDIA

Chapter 2

SpaceX: https://www.spacex.com/news/2005/12/19/june-2005-december-2005

Chapter 3

SpaceX: https://twitter.com/spaccx/status/1473236198722179072?lang=en

Elon Musk: https://twitter.com/elonmusk/status/936782477502246912?lang=en-GB

Elon Musk: https://twitter.com/elonmusk/status/972628124893671432?lang=en

Elon Musk: https://twitter.com/elonmusk/status/1186523464712146944?ref_src=twsrc%5Etfw

Chapter 4

Elon Musk: https://twitter.com/elonmusk/status/1367611973697818628?ref_src=twsrc%5Etfw%7Ctwcamp%5Etweetembed%7Ctwterm%5E1367835377101381637%7Ctwgr%5E%7Ctwcon%5Es3_&ref_url=https%3A%2F%2Fwww.stuff.co.nz%2Fmotoring%2F124464735%2Felon-musk-trolls-gm-chrysler-on-twitter-ford-ceo-responds-with-one-word

Elon Musk (7 August 2018). 'Taking Tesla Private': https://www.tesla.com/blog/taking-tesla-private?redirect=no

Elon Musk: https://twitter.com/elonmusk/status/1499976967105433600

Elon Musk: https://twitter.com/elonmusk/status/1047943670350020608

Elon Musk: https://twitter.com/28delayslater/status/1492112762474057729

Elon Musk: https://twitter.com/elonmusk/status/1423156475799683075?lang=en-GB

Elon Musk: https://twitter.com/elonmusk/
    status/1433474893316722691?lang=en

Parag Agrawal: https://twitter.com/paraga/
    status/1513354622466867201

Elon Musk: https://twitter.com/elonmusk/status/1511322655609303043

Elon Musk: https://twitter.com/elonmusk/
    status/1507259709224632344

Elon Musk: https://twitter.com/elonmusk/
    status/1507907130124222471

Elon Musk: https://twitter.com/elonmusk/status/1511143607385874434

Chapter 5

Elon Musk: https://twitter.com/elonmusk/
    status/1500613952031444995?ref_src=twsrc%5
    Etfw%7Ctwcamp%5Etweetembed%7Ctwterm%5E15006
    13952031444995%7Ctwgr%5E%7Ctwcon%5Es1_&ref_
    url=https%3A%2F%2Fwww.businessinsider.com%2Felon-musk-
    nuclear-energy-europe-russia-oil-gas-supply-crunch-2022-3

Elon Musk: https://twitter.com/elonmusk/status/810108760010043392

Chapter 6

Elon Musk: https://www.reddit.com/r/IAmA/comments/2rgsan/i_am_
    elon_musk_ceocto_of_a_rocket_company_ama/

Jim Cantrell: https://www.quora.com/profile/Jim-Cantrell

Elon Musk: https://twitter.com/elonmusk/
    status/1324736076800577537?ref_src=twsrc%5Etfw

Conclusion

Elon Musk: https://twitter.com/elonmusk/
    status/1379887294933467139?lang=en

VIDEOS

Chapter 1

Joe Rogan Experience #1169 – Elon Musk: https://www.youtube.com/watch?v=ycPr5-27vSI&t=599s

Elon Musk talks about his upbringing: https://www.youtube.com/watch?v=0nwbRT3Knv8

Chapter 2

Elon Musk – History of Zip2: https://www.youtube.com/watch?v=7sLmeYNmZKY

'Too many MBAs ruining companies,' Elon Musk explains: https://www.youtube.com/watch?v=Y6P8qdanszw

Watch a young Elon Musk get his first supercar in 1999, *CNN Business*: https://edition.cnn.com/videos/business/2021/01/07/elon-musk-gets-his-mclaren-supercar-1999-vault-orig.cnn

Elon Musk talks about getting fired as PayPal CEO (2008): https://www.youtube.com/watch?v=wKacw4zHj-Q

Elon Musk: 'The government is simply the biggest corporation, with the monopoly on violence.': https://www.youtube.com/watch?v=-_wvTa8aiu8

Chapter 3

Elon Musk in conversation at Tesla Motors | 18 March 2013: https://www.youtube.com/watch?v=IJauyGO5fiw&t=282s

Elon Musk – People Don't Realize What's Coming!: https://www.youtube.com/watch?v=1wotmu1KL0E

Making Life Multiplanetary: https://www.youtube.com/watch?v=tdUX3ypDVwI&t=724s

Making Humans a Multiplanetary Species: https://www.youtube.com/watch?v=H7Uyfqi_TE8

Chapter 4

Elon Musk – Is Global Warming Real?: https://www.youtube.com/watch?v=_ozlbGB57aE

Elon Musk Just Revealed His GENIUS Marketing Strategy!: https://www.youtube.com/watch?v=z2lHoskBaeM

Elon Musk about politics: https://www.youtube.com/watch?v=eo1_TvDCMw4

Elon Musk: Self-driving is way harder than I thought | Lex Fridman Podcast Clips: https://www.youtube.com/watch?v=MyLUiE-XfQI

Chapter 5

Elon Musk - Solar is the Future: https://www.youtube.com/watch?v=DB_zSKJDGpU

'Watch Before They DELETE This!' - Elon Musk's URGENT WARNING (2022): https://www.youtube.com/watch?v=K5LeI7l1_ko

Clubhouse Elon Musk interview transcript: https://www.youtube.com/watch?v=wqD4X5ABgi8&t=2s

Elon Musk Wants to Revolutionize Education: https://www.youtube.com/watch?v=sXdfRYyzbmU

Chapter 6

An Evening – Elon Musk VS Alison van Diggelen – Science Debate: https://www.youtube.com/watch?v=Wwk-BXA14Ec

The First Principles Method Explained by Elon Musk: https://www.youtube.com/watch?v=NV3sBlRgzTI&t=4s

Elon Musk: SpaceX, Mars, Tesla Autopilot, Self-Driving, Robotics, and AI | Lex Fridman Podcast #252: https://www.youtube.com/watch?v=DxREm3s1scA

Elon Musk: Limbic System, Cerebral Cortex, and a Tertiary Layer of Digital Super-Intelligence: https://www.youtube.com/watch?v=4Ei7MQjRK0U

"REFRAME Your THINKING!" | Elon Musk (@elonmusk): https://www.youtube.com/watch?v=5mtGdIsHxyU

TAKES RISKS NOW - Elon Musk [THE BEST]: https://www.youtube.com/watch?v=00cizszd4z0

Conclusion

Joe Rogan Experience #1470 – Elon Musk: https://www.youtube.com/watch?v=RcYjXbSJBN8

WEBSITES

SpaceX: https://www.spacex.com
– https://www.spacex.com/vehicles/dragon/
– https://www.spacex.com/vehicles/falcon-heavy/

Tesla: https://www.tesla.com
– https://www.tesla.com/en_GB/blog/mythbusters-part-2-tesla-roadster-not-converted-lotus-elise
– https://www.tesla.com/en_gb/cybertruck
– https://www.tesla.com/blog/secret-tesla-motors-master-plan-just-between-you-and-me
– https://www.tesla.com/en_GB/blog/master-plan-part-deux

US Securities and Exchange Commission: https://www.investor.gov/
– https://www.investor.gov/introduction-investing/investing-basics/role-sec
– https://www.sec.gov/news/press-release/2018-226

The Boring Company: https://www.boringcompany.com/
– https://www.boringcompany.com/lvcc

– https://www.boringcompany.com/vegas-loop
– https://www.boringcompany.com/prufrock

OpenAi: https://openai.com/
– https://openai.com/research/

Neuralink: https://neuralink.com/
– https://neuralink.com/about/
– https://neuralink.com/applications/

Astra Nova School: https://www.astranova.org/
– https://www.astranova.org/xyz/synthesis

LEGAL DOCUMENTS

SEC v. Elon Musk, No. 1:18-cv-8865-AJN; *SEC v. Tesla, Inc.*,
    No. 1:18-cv-8947-AJN (17 February 2022): https://storage.
    courtlistener.com/recap/gov.uscourts.nysd.501881/gov.uscourts.
    nysd.501881.24.0.pdf

United States Securities and Exchange Commission: – https://www.sec.
    gov/ix?doc=/Archives/edgar/data/0001318605/00009501702200079
    6/tsla-20211231.htm#legal_proceedings

Department of the Treasury: Internal Revenue Service: https://www.
    documentcloud.org/documents/4501290-2015-E990-for-Ad-Astra.
    html

INDEX